Brontë at home

baking from the
SCANDI KITCHEN

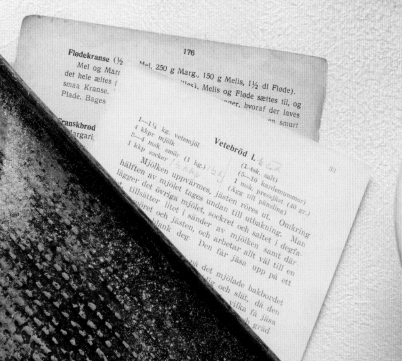

Brontë at home

baking from the
SCANDI KITCHEN

Brontë Aurell

Photography by Peter Cassidy

RYLAND PETERS & SMALL
LONDON • NEW YORK

First published in 2019 by
Ryland Peters & Small
20–21 Jockey's Fields
London WC1R 4BW
and
341 E 116th St
New York NY 10029
www.rylandpeters.com

Some of the recipes in this book have been
previously published by Ryland Peters & Small.

ISBN: 978-1-78879-151-9

10 9 8 7 6 5 4 3 2 1

Printed and bound in China.

CIP data from the Library of Congress has been
applied for. A CIP record for this book is available
from the British Library.

Notes
* Both British (metric) and American (imperial plus
US cups) are included in these recipes; however, it
is important to work with one set of measurements
and not alternate between the two within a recipe.
* All butter should be unsalted unless specified.
* All eggs are medium (UK) or large (US), unless
specified as large, in which case US extra large
should be used. Uncooked or partially cooked eggs
should not be served to the very old, frail, young
children, pregnant women or those with
compromised immune systems.
* Ovens should be preheated to the specified
temperatures. We recommend using an oven
thermometer. If using a fan-assisted oven, adjust
temperatures according to the manufacturer's
instructions.
* When a recipe calls for the grated zest of citrus
fruit, buy unwaxed fruit and wash well before
using. If you can only find treated fruit, scrub well
in warm, soapy water before using.

Dedication
For David Jørgensen

Senior Designer
Sonya Nathoo

Editor
Miriam Catley

Head of Production
Patricia Harrington

Art Director
Leslie Harrington

Editorial Director
Julia Charles

Publisher
Cindy Richards

Food Stylist
Kathy Kordalis

Assistant Food Stylist
Anna Hiddleston

Prop Stylist
Tony Hutchinson

Indexer
Vanessa Bird

contents

introduction

The connection between food and memory is wonderful. As I have grown older, I realize so many of my dearest memories are hidden inside tastes and smells, allowing me to be instantly transported back to a moment in time where even people now long gone are still there. Biting into a warm bun, fresh out of the oven, can transport me back to my grandmother's kitchen, to her warm smile and her hugs. Removing a hot apple pie from the oven allows me to connect with my mother, even if she is an ocean away.

My kitchen in London may be small, but it already holds a hundred food memories of my children and I baking on rainy days, creating new recipes, learning about what works (and often what doesn't). Dancing to 80s playlists and laughing, as we taste batter, crack eggs and as I try to impart some skills that will help them in the future when they begin their own kitchen stories. In that kitchen, we live, we love and we learn. To me, comfort baking is a wonderful time machine and a memory maker, all in one.

The Scandinavian word 'hygge' is one that really comes to life when you add a good home bake to the mix. Hygge simply means enjoying the moment you're in, while you are in it – and this magic often happens when we sit together and share food, especially sweet things. Hygge and comfort is in that warm, sticky cinnamon bun fresh out of the oven. It's in the softness of a cake, it's in the velvety feel of vanilla cream. Hygge is when we bake because of the sheer joy of it: creating something for someone we love to evoke feelings of comfort.

Baking is personal. Sure, you can buy the most beautiful looking cake from the window of a patisserie and you can cover things in icing and make them look pretty, but you will never, ever be able to beat the feeling of real comfort that can only happen when someone has baked and created something with love. Because baking at home is all about that: it's about creating and eating to please people around you. There is something really wonderful in that, which no money can buy, no matter how rustic the result may be.

This book contains a selection of my favourite recipes from my previous books as well as a stack of new ones. All these recipes have been baked in my little kitchen with my daughters, Astrid and Elsa. We had a lot of fun and made a huge mess. My wish is that your version of this book gets sticky pages and that you find a few recipes from which to create your own memory magic.

Love,
Brontë x

the baking pantry

Scandinavia is a huge place, so what defines an ingredient as 'local' varies from hilly Norway to flat Denmark – there's a 2,500 km/1,500 miles distance between them. However, we all share a love for lots of similar products, so here is a brief guide to some of the products you will need for Nordic baking. We've put this together based on things we get asked for at the café, and we often help people source specific ingredients or find local replacements to use instead. You will find a more comprehensive list at www.scandikitchen.co.uk.

POPULAR SPICES

Cardamom/kardemomme/kardemumma
It was actually the Vikings who first sampled this spice during their raids on Constantinople. We use the ground variety, which you can buy in larger supermarkets and Asian speciality shops. I favour using freshly ground cardamom, though, because it is one of those spices that loses potency very quickly when pre-ground. If you use freshly ground, watch the quantity, as it is strong and if you are not used to the punchy flavour, hold back a bit. To make ground cardamom at home, either buy cardamom seeds online and finely grind in a spice grinder or pestle and mortar, or open the pods (Scandinavians prefer the green pods) and scoop out the seeds to grind (remove the little woody bits of husk inside the pod and only grind the seeds).

Cinnamon/kanel
Where would the Nordic people be without their beloved cinnamon buns? We use cinnamon in a lot of our baking, from biscuits to cakes and breads. There are different grades of cinnamon – go for good-quality ground cinnamon.

Cloves/nelliker/kryddnejlika/nellik
We use both whole cloves and ground cloves in our baking, especially at Christmas, when whole cloves are used in mulled wine and ground cloves are essential in ginger cookies.

Fennel seeds/fennikel frø/fänkålsfrön
We use fennel seeds mainly in bread – both for loaves and as a flavouring for crispbread.

Ginger/ingefær/ingefära
Ground ginger is commonly used in ginger cookies and soft ginger cake, but also in some other cakes. Whole dried ginger is essential in mulled wine.

Liquorice/lakrids/lakrits
While we have a long history full of love for liquorice, it is only in recent years we have started to bake with it. This is largely due to great brands of purist liquorice coming to the market, such as Lakrids by Bülow from Denmark and Lakritsfabrikken in Sweden. Either the powder or liquorice syrup is used in most sweet recipes. In some Swedish recipes it can be referred to as Hockey Pulver.

Salt
The Nordics have been preserving food in salt for centuries and we love salty foods, both savoury and sweet. We add salt to many cookies and cakes and we love salty liquorice. We use ammonium chloride for flavouring our liquorice, also known as salmiakki. It is an acquired taste – but once you get the taste for things such as salty liquorice, a life-long addiction usually starts. You have been warned.

Saffron/safran/saffran

People in Sweden and Norway use saffron during the month of December in traditional Lucia buns. We commonly use ground saffron, which you can buy in specialist shops (ask behind the counter, as it is usually kept behind the till). If you are using strands, grind these before use. To intensify the colour, soak in warm liquid before using.

Seville orange peel/pomerans

We use this in our mulled wine and dried in some Christmas breads and biscuits. You can substitute with normal dried orange peel, but the flavour will not be as subtle or bitter.

Vanilla/vanilje/vanilj

Scandinavian recipes often call for vanilla sugar, which is a quick and easy substitute for whole vanilla pods/beans. You can make your own at home by adding 250 ml/1 cup of icing/confectioners' sugar to a food processor or spice grinder with two vanilla pods/beans – dried-out hard ones are fine – a great way to use these up. Pulse until pulverized, then sift out the large pieces of peel. You can buy vanilla sugar in any Scandinavian food shops, too – Tørsleff is a great brand. You can, of course, also always substitute with vanilla extract or real vanilla pods/beans.

BERRIES

Cloudberries/multebær/hjortron

Fresh cloudberries are rare. They grow wild near the Arctic Circle and their season lasts around three weeks in July and August. They are hard to cultivate and foragers don't tend to part with information freely! Frozen cloudberries are easier to get hold of, but they are expensive. A little goes a long way; this is a gourmet berry, even to the Scandinavians. Most Scandinavian shops will stock cloudberry jam/jelly, which can be used in most of our baking recipes.

The cloudberry is very tart and the jam is not used as a spread for toast, as it is far too expensive. Use it with strong cheese or in desserts (it's particularly great heated up and poured over vanilla ice cream).

Lingonberries/tyttebær/lingon

Norwegians, Finns and Swedes will have lingonberries in their freezers throughout the year; fresh ones are picked in August. We also have lingonberry jam/jelly and compotes in our store cupboards. You can use the frozen or fresh berries for baking, and you can also use the jam/jelly for some cakes or cookies. If you cannot get hold of lingonberries, substitute with cranberries or raspberries, depending on the recipe. Many Scandinavian shops sell the frozen berries.

GRAINS AND FLOURS

Oats/havregryn

Used in porridge, granola, muesli and baking. We also eat raw oats with milk for breakfast. Oat flakes (jumbo oats) or cut oats are favoured.

Potato flour/kartoffelmel/potatismjöl/potetmel

You can buy this in speciality stores. Once potato starch is added, the dish should not boil (especially in fruit-based sauces as these will go cloudy after boiling).

Rye flour rugmel/rågmjöl

There are two kinds of rye flour sold in supermarkets. Wholegrain rye and light (sifted) rye. Light rye flour is often called Type 997. It is, basically, sifted wholegrain rye flour, so if you are pushed, you can sift the dark rye flour before using in a recipe.

Rye flour mix/sigtemel/rågsikt

In Sweden and Denmark, rågsikt (sigtemel in Danish) is very common. It's 60% white wheat flour and 40% light rye (type 997), sifted. You can make this at home by mixing the same quantities.

Rye flakes/rugflager/rågflingor

I love using rye flakes in granola, flapjacks and porridge (mixed with normal oats) for their nutty flavour and a good bite. Available in health food stores, they take longer to cook and are quite chewy. If you are using oats in a recipe, consider mixing part oats, part rye flakes.

Semolina/semuljegryn/mannagryn/semulegryn

Used for some desserts and also as a porridge.

Spelt flour/speltmel/dinkelmjöl

This is an older type of wheat grain and less refined. You can get both white and wholegrain spelt flour – we use both in this book. Spelt contains less gluten than other wheat flours.

YEAST AND LEAVENERS

Baker's ammonia/hartshorn powder/hjortetakssalt/hjorthornssalt

Used in old Nordic recipes to ensure cookies rise and get crispy at lower temperatures, baker's ammonia gives off a very strong ammonia smell as you bake, but this disappears as soon as the cookies cool.

You can buy it online or at some pharmacies, as well as in many Scandinavian food shops. It was traditionally made from the ground antlers of young stags, but nowadays it's all chemical. When using baker's ammonia, don't eat the raw dough. Substitute with baking powder, although the result will not be as crispy.

Dry active yeast

Little yeast granules you have to activate in lukewarm water before using. This is the next best thing to fresh yeast. Activate and leave for 15 minutes in the finger-warm liquid to go frothy and bubbly – then use in the recipe as normal.

Fresh yeast

25 g/1 oz. of fresh yeast (also known as compressed yeast) is the equivalent to 13 g/½ oz. of dry active yeast. It usually comes in packs of 50 g/2 oz. and looks a bit like clay. Take care not to kill fresh yeast with hot liquid or by adding salt to the yeast before the flour.

If you use heavier flours, such as rye, the yeast takes a long time to lift it and you will have denser breads. Consider mixing lighter flours with the darker ones if you want fluffy loaves.

Instant dried yeast

If you have no option but to use instant dry yeast (a fine powder sold in sachets), skip the adding to liquid step and add to the dry ingredients. Follow the manufacturer's guidelines for equivalent measures.

OTHER STUFF

Marzipan/marsipan

We use ready-made marzipan in a lot of our baking recipes and have included an easy recipe to make your own 50/50 marzipan (see page 15). In the UK and America, marzipan is commonly only 25% almonds).

You can keep leftover marzipan in the fridge for a week or so. You can bind it with water instead of egg white if you are worried about eating raw egg white, but I think it is nicer when egg white is used and easier to work with.

Punch

A type of Swedish rum liquor often used to flavour rum truffle treats such as Romkugler (see page 32) – you can substitute with good concentrated rum flavourings for baked treats if you prefer.

basic recipes

These recipes are referred to in various recipes throughout the book. They are good staples and can be mixed and matched with other ingredients.

layer cake bases

This recipe is similar to a very light Génoise sponge. Some people use baking powder in layer cakes, but I opt to use just eggs and sugar as the leavener because I feel the end result is more delicate. The secret is to whip the eggs and sugar properly to ribbon stage. Secondly, when you fold in the flour, do so very gently in figure-of-eight folds.

4 eggs
120 g/²/₃ cup caster/granulated sugar
120 g/²/₃ cup plus 2 tablespoons plain/all-purpose flour or cake flour
a pinch of salt

1 teaspoon vanilla sugar OR extract OR use the seeds of 1 vanilla pod/bean
25 g/¹/₄ stick butter, melted and set aside to cool

3 baking sheets

Preheat the oven to 180°C (350°F) Gas 4.

Beat together the eggs and sugar on high speed in a stand mixer or using a hand-held electric whisk. Beat until the mixture reaches ribbon stage – you will be able to see the traces of the mixture when you move the whisk.

Use a 20-cm/8-inch diameter plate to draw three circles on baking parchment. Cut these out and place one parchment circle on each of the three baking sheets. Set aside.

Combine the flour, salt and vanilla in a separate bowl. Sift into the egg mixture, bit by bit, carefully folding using a figure-of-eight movement until incorporated. Pour the cooled melted butter down the side of the bowl and fold carefully again, trying not to knock out air.

Divide the mixture evenly between the parchment circles on the baking sheets, spreading right to the edges of each circle with the back of a spoon. If they go over a bit, don't worry, you can cut these bits off afterwards.

Bake in the preheated oven for about 5–7 minutes or until light golden brown. Remove from the oven and allow to cool before removing the baking parchment. If the parchment sticks, slightly dampen the paper side with cold water and the paper will come off easily. Trim any untidy edges using a sharp knife.

Note: If you really want to use baking powder to guarantee a rise, add 1 teaspoon to the flour for a slight lift.

danish pastry

Many people are scared to attempt Danish pastry from scratch. It is, admittedly, a little time-consuming, but it isn't actually hard – it is so worth it once you taste those flaky pastries, straight from the oven.

25 g/1 oz. fresh yeast or 13 g/2½ teaspoons dried/active dry yeast
150 ml/²/₃ cup whole milk, heated to 36–37°C (97–98°F)
50 g/¼ cup caster/granulated sugar
50 g/3½ tablespoons butter, softened
350 g/2½ cups strong white/bread flour, plus extra for dusting

1 teaspoon salt
1 egg plus 1 egg yolk

FILLING
350 g/3 sticks butter, softened
25 g/3 tablespoons plain/all-purpose flour

a baking sheet, lined with baking parchment

If you are using fresh yeast, add the yeast and whole milk to a stand mixer with a dough hook attached. Mix until the yeast has dissolved. If using dried/active dry yeast, pour the milk into a bowl, sprinkle over the yeast and whisk together. Cover with clingfilm/plastic wrap and leave in a warm place for about 15 minutes to activate and become frothy and bubbly. Pour into the mixer with the dough hook attached. Stir in the sugar and softened butter, then mix the flour with the salt and start to add, bit by bit. Add the egg halfway through along with the remaining flour. Keep mixing with the dough hook for 5 minutes. The resulting dough should still be a bit sticky. Cover the bowl with clingfilm/plastic wrap and leave to rise for an hour or until doubled in size.

Turn the dough out onto a floured surface and knead through, adding more flour as needed until you have a stretchy, workable dough. Roll the dough out into a big square 35 x 35 cm/ 14 x 14 inches or as evenly as you can.

For the filling, mix the butter with the flour into a just mouldable ball using your hands. It's important this mixture is a similar consistency to the dough. If your hands are too warm, use a rolling pin and beat the butter flat between two sheets of baking parchment. Flatten the butter out to a square 25 x 25 cm/9¾ x 9¾ inches then place this butter square onto your dough at a 45° angle so that the dough corners can fold back in to cover the butter, like an envelope. Fold the dough corners over the butter until you have completely enclosed it. Dust with flour and roll out the package to a rectangle around 30 x 50 cm/11¾ x 20 inches then fold the layers the short way twice so you end up with a rectangle approx. 30 x 15 cm/11¾ x 6 inches (3 layers with butter). It is important that you roll carefully so that the butter stays inside the pastry package.

Place the dough on the prepared baking sheet, cover with clingfilm/plastic wrap and chill for 15 minutes in the refrigerator. Repeat the folding process: roll to a rectangle and fold back on itself – you now have nine layers of butter. Again, rest the dough in the fridge for 15 minutes, then repeat the rolling process again so you end up with yet another rectangle in three folds with 27 layers of butter in total. After a final rest in the refrigerator, your pastry is now ready to shape into whatever you want to bake.

sweet shortcrust pastry

This basic sweet shortcrust pastry is useful for many recipes in this book. If you prefer a less sweet base, simply reduce the sugar content slightly. Remember that keeping the butter as cold as possible is key to making pastry with a good short texture.

- 200 g/1¾ sticks cold butter, cubed
- 350 g/2⅔ cups plain/all-purpose flour
- 125 g/1 cup plus 1 tablespoon icing/confectioners' sugar
- 1 teaspoon vanilla extract OR seeds from ½ a vanilla pod/bean
- 1 egg

MAKES 700 G/1½ LB. DOUGH

Rub the cold butter into the flour until sandy in texture, then add the icing/confectioners' sugar and vanilla. Add the whole egg and mix until the dough holds together and becomes smooth, taking care not to over-mix. You can also make the dough in the food processor by pulsing the ingredients together briefly, if you wish. Wrap the dough in clingfilm/plastic wrap and chill for at least 30 minutes in the refrigerator before using.

pastry cream

There is something so deliciously decadent about cakes with pastry cream. The comfort of custard, I usually call it. I love making it from scratch and use it for anything from filling cakes to layering trifles.

- 500 ml/2 cups plus 2 tablespoons whole milk
- 1 vanilla pod/bean, seeds scraped
- 1 whole egg plus 1 egg yolk
- 100 g/½ cup caster/superfine sugar
- 30 g/¼ cup cornflour/cornstarch
- ½ teaspoon salt
- 25 g/1¾ tablespoons butter

MAKES ABOUT 600–625 G/21–22 OZ.

In a saucepan, heat the milk with the scraped out seeds from the vanilla pod/bean.

In a separate bowl, whisk together the egg and yolk and sugar and add the cornflour/cornstarch.

When the milk has just reached boiling point, take off the heat and pour one third into the egg mixture while whisking continuously.

Once whisked through, pour the egg mixture back into the remaining hot milk. Return to the stove and bring to the boil, carefully. Whisk continuously as the mixture thickens, for just under a minute, then remove from the heat and stir in the salt and butter.

Pour into a cold bowl and place a sheet of baking parchment on top to prevent the cream from forming a crust as it cools. The mixture will keep well in the refrigerator for a few days.

marzipan (for baking)

I often use store-bought marzipan as long as it is minimum 50% almond content. But sometimes it can be hard to get hold off and making your own is simple. This recipe contains raw egg white. If you're not going to be cooking it, use a hot sugar syrup instead of egg.

200 g/2 cups finely ground almonds (if the grind feels coarse, re-grind it at home a few times in your processor)

100 g/½ cup caster/granulated sugar

100 g/⅔ cup icing/confectioners' sugar

1 teaspoon almond extract

1 egg white (approx. 30 g/1 oz.) ideally pasteurized

MAKES ABOUT 400 G/14 OZ.

Blend the ingredients together in a food processor until you have a smooth marzipan.

Roll the mixture into a log and wrap tightly in clingfilm/plastic wrap. Chill in the refrigerator for at least 1 hour before using.

Variation
Pistachio Marzipan – substitute raw pistachios and pistachio essence (available in middle eastern delis and online) for the ground almonds and almond extract.

remonce almond paste

This is a classic almond-based filling for Danish pastries. It is nearly always baked rather than used raw and is integral to many Nordic cake and pastry recipes. Sometimes, cinnamon, vanilla and dark brown sugar are added (for cinnamon swirls and buns, for example). Remonce is sometimes translated to Lord Mayor's filling, although I've never heard this term used in the UK.

100 g/3½ oz. marzipan (minimum 50% store-bought or see recipe above)

100 g/7 tablespoons butter, softened

100 g/¾ cup plus

1½ tablespoons icing/confectioners' sugar, sifted

MAKES ABOUT 300 G/10½ OZ.

Grate the marzipan into a bowl.

Add the softened butter and icing/confectioners' sugar.

Whisk everything together until smooth. Your remonce paste is now ready to use.

cookies &
small treats

nordic ginger biscuits
pepparkakor

Ginger biscuits are not just for Christmas, but of course, in every Scandinavian home you will find mountains of these all throughout the festive season. Each country has regional variations and names, but the main ingredients are the same.

550 g/4 cups plain/ all-purpose flour
1 teaspoon bicarbonate of/ baking soda
1 teaspoon ground ginger
1 teaspoon ground cloves
2 teaspoons ground cinnamon
1 teaspoon ground cardamom
a pinch of ground allspice
a pinch of salt
150 g/1 stick plus 2 tablespoons butter, room temperature

200 g/ 10 tablespoons golden/light corn syrup
100 g/½ cup caster/ granulated sugar
100 g/½ cup dark brown sugar
150 ml/²/₃ cup double/heavy cream
icing/confectioners' sugar, to dust

baking sheets lined with baking parchment

MAKES 50–70

Mix the flour and bicarbonate of/baking soda with the dry spices and salt. Add the butter and all the other ingredients and mix until you have an even dough. It may still be sticky, but shape into a log and wrap in clingfilm/plastic wrap and leave to rest in the fridge overnight before using.

Preheat the oven to 200°C (400°F) Gas 6.

Roll out the dough thinly on a floured surface and use cookie cutters to cut your desired shapes. You want the biscuits/cookies to be thin. Arrange on the prepared baking sheet.

Bake in the preheated oven – each batch will take 5–6 minutes depending on the thickness. You want the biscuits/cookies to be a darker shade of brown.

Remove from the oven and cool on a cooling rack. Dust with icing/confectioners' sugar and serve or keep in an airtight container.

Variations
Orange Pepparkakor – add the grated zest of 1 orange.

Cedar – these are known as French Ginger biscuits in Sweden, or 'old-fashioned ginger biscuits' – add a few drops of food grade essential cedarwood oil.

Lemon – add the grated zest from ½ lemon and a few drops lemon oil.

Almond – add finely chopped almonds and instead of rolling out and using cookie cutters, simply roll into logs and slice the dough when really cold.

finnish biscuits
finska pinnar

These shortbread are called Finnish Biscuits, except the Danes claim
to have invented them around the 1900s – but the Swedes claim the
same, so, someone, somewhere, is telling porkies. In Finland, there is
an old biscuit that is somewhat similar called Mantelikeksit, so it may
have origins from there and then been adapted locally. That aside,
these are lovely little treats – often made around Christmastime.

175 g/1½ sticks cold
   butter, cubed
250 g/1¾ cups plus
   2 tablespoons
   plain/all-purpose
   flour
50 g/½ cup ground
   almonds
50 g/¼ cup caster/
   granulated sugar
1 egg yolk
2 teaspoons
   almond extract
1 teaspoon vanilla
   extract

TOPPING
50 g/scant ½ cup
   blanched,
   chopped
   almonds
50 g/1¾ oz. pearl/
   nibbed sugar
1 egg white

a baking sheet,
   lined with baking
   parchment

MAKES 30

In a food processor, pulse the butter and flour with
the ground almonds and sugar until well mixed. Next
add the egg yolk, almond extract and vanilla extract and
pulse until the dough sticks together and is smooth. Rest
in the fridge for a minimum of 30 minutes.

Preheat the oven to 180°C (350°F) Gas 4.

Put the pearl/nibbed sugar and the chopped almonds
in a bowl and mix well.

Roll the dough into 4 x 45 x 50 cm/18 x 20 in. logs. Cut
into pieces approx. 5 cm/2 in. (each about 20 g/¾ oz.). Dip
one side in the egg white and then press into the nut/
sugar mixture, flattening the biscuits as you do so. Put
on the prepared baking sheet, nut/sugar-side up and
repeat for the remaining pieces.

Bake in the preheated oven for about 8–11 minutes until
just browned at the sides. Transfer to a wire rack and
leave to cool completely. Store in an airtight container.

Note: You can vary the flavours by using different nuts
– pistachio goes very well.

norwegian butter cookies
serinakaker

Christmastime in Norway always calls for home baking. The tradition of baking at least seven kinds of cookies for Christmas still holds true – but the handy thing is that a lot of these have a similar base dough, so the work isn't too taxing. These traditional butter cookies are quick to make and taste delicious.

300 g/2¼ cups plain/all-purpose flour
1 tablespoon baking powder
a pinch of salt
200 g/¾ cup plus 2 tablespoons cold butter, cut into cubes
125 g/¾ cup plus 2 tablespoons icing/confectioners' sugar

2 teaspoons vanilla sugar
1 egg
1 egg white, beaten, for brushing
pearl/nibbed sugar or chopped almonds, for sprinkling

baking sheets, greased and lined with baking parchment

MAKES ABOUT 40

Mix the flour with the baking powder and a pinch of salt in a bowl and add the cubed butter. Mix with your fingers until it forms crumbs, then add the icing/confectioners' sugar and vanilla sugar and mix again. Add the whole egg and mix until the dough is even (but don't overmix).

Pop the dough into a food bag and leave to settle in the fridge for about an hour.

Preheat the oven to 180°C (350°F) Gas 4.

Cut the dough into around 40 equal pieces (around 15 g/½ oz. each), roll them into small balls, and place on the prepared baking sheets. Make sure to leave space around each piece of dough, as they spread out while baking. Using the back of a fork, press each one down gently in the middle to a diameter of around 3 cm/1¼ in. (they will spread more when baking). If you prefer a flat surface, use the bottom of a glass or similar.

Brush the biscuits with the egg white and sprinkle the pearl sugar or chopped almonds over the top.

Bake in the preheated oven for around 10 minutes or until just baked through (don't let them go brown – you want only a slight tinge of colour at the edges). Baking times can vary depending on your oven, so keep an eye on them.

Remove from the oven and leave to cool on a wire rack before transferring to an airtight container.

vanilla rings
vaniliekranse

Every Danish family has a recipe for these little vanilla wreath cookies. The dough has to be quite cold to work with in order to achieve the ridges on the final cookies, but it can be quite tricky to extract the dough from the piping bag. I tend to use a large piping nozzle and press the dough through with my finger, one at a time.

170 g/³⁄₄ cup plus 1½ tablespoons caster/granulated sugar
200 g/³⁄₄ cup plus 2 tablespoons butter, at room temperature
275 g/2 cups strong white/bread flour
100 g/1 cup ground almonds
1 teaspoon baking powder

1 egg
a pinch of salt
seeds from 1 vanilla pod/bean

a strong piping/pastry bag and a medium star nozzle/tip
baking sheets, greased and lined with baking parchment

MAKES ABOUT 30

Mix the sugar and butter (only briefly until just combined), then add the remaining ingredients and mix until you have an even dough (you can do this in a food processor or by hand). Do not over-mix. Your dough needs to be soft enough to push through a piping/pastry bag nozzle/tip. It is a hard dough – in Denmark, most people use a metal case to push the dough through the nozzle/tip. A fabric piping/pastry bag is also good. If you find it really hard but have a good-sized nozzle, you can simply push the dough through with your thumb.

Pipe out the dough 8–10 cm/3¼–4 in. long, then carefully connect into circles and place on the prepared baking sheets. Make sure the dough is no thicker than your little finger, because they will spread a bit during baking. Put the baking sheets in the fridge if you have space for about 30 minutes before baking.

Preheat the oven to 200°C (400°F) Gas 6.

Put a chilled baking sheet of cookies in the preheated oven and bake for 8–10 minutes, or until the slightest tinge of golden brown appears at the edges. Remove from the oven and allow to cool before eating. Repeat until everything is baked. Transfer to a wire rack and leave to cool completely. Store in an airtight container.

Variation
Add the grated zest of one orange for a citrus flavour.

chocolate biscuit slices
chokladsnittar

These moreish biscuits/cookies are easy to make and bake in super-quick time – the perfect accompaniment to a cup of coffee.

100 g/1 stick minus 1 tablespoon butter, softened
80 g/⅓ cup plus 1 tablespoon caster/granulated sugar
2 teaspoons vanilla sugar
1 teaspoon golden syrup/light corn syrup
150 g/1 cup plus 2 tablespoons plain/all-purpose flour
4 teaspoons cacao or cocoa powder
1 teaspoon baking powder
pearl/nibbed sugar or chopped almonds, to decorate

2 baking sheets, greased and lined with baking parchment

MAKES 24

Preheat the oven to 180°C (350°F) Gas 4.

In a bowl, cream together the butter, caster/granulated sugar and vanilla sugar. Add the syrup and mix well. In a separate bowl, sift the dry ingredients together, then mix into the wet mixture. Bring the mixture together with your hands to form an even dough – it should not be sticky. Split the dough into two lumps. Roll out each lump into a 6 x 35 cm/2½ x 14 in. rectangle, directly on the prepared baking sheets.

Sprinkle the pearl sugar or chopped almonds down the middle of the dough, then bake in the preheated oven for about 10 minutes until almost baked through. As soon as you remove them from the oven, use a pizza wheel or sharp knife to cut each piece into 12 even-sized strips. Leave to cool on a wire rack and store in an airtight container for up to a week.

toffee biscuit slices
kolasnittar

A Swedish classic, these toffee biscuits/cookies are super-quick to make. We like adding flakes of sea salt to the top, but you can easily leave this out, if you wish.

140 g/1¼ sticks butter
120 g/⅔ cup minus 1 tablespoon caster/granulated sugar
4 tablespoons golden syrup/light corn syrup
1½ teaspoons vanilla sugar
1 teaspoon baking powder
300 g/2¼ cups plain/all-purpose flour
½ teaspoon sea salt (optional)

3 baking sheets, greased and lined with baking parchment

MAKES 36

Preheat the oven to 180°C (350°F) Gas 4.

In a bowl, cream the butter and caster/granulated sugar until pale and fluffy, then add the syrup, followed by the vanilla sugar, baking powder and flour. Mix with your hands until you have an even dough.

Cut the dough into three equal pieces. Roll out to the size of 6 x 35 cm/2½ x 14 in. directly on the prepared baking sheets. Sprinkle the salt over the top of the dough, if using.

Bake in the preheated oven for 8–10 minutes. As soon as you remove the biscuits/cookies from the oven, use a pizza wheel or sharp knife to cut each rectangle into 12 pieces.

Leave to cool on a wire rack and store in an airtight container for up to a week.

daim cookies
daimkakor

150 g/1¼ sticks butter
300 g/2¼ cups plain/all-purpose flour
½ teaspoon bicarbonate of/baking soda
½ teaspoon vanilla sugar OR extract OR the seeds from 1 vanilla pod/bean
¼ teaspoon sea salt
150 g/¾ cup light brown soft sugar
100 g/½ cup caster/granulated sugar
1 whole egg plus 1 egg yolk
2 tablespoons whole milk
5 Daim bars (28 g/1 oz. each), roughly chopped

2 baking sheets, greased and lined with baking parchment

MAKES 20–22 COOKIES

Melt the butter and set aside to cool. Combine the flour, bicarbonate of/baking soda, vanilla and salt in a bowl and set aside.

Combine the sugars with the cooled, melted butter and stir until no lumps remain. Combine the egg, egg yolk and milk and mix with the sugar and butter until thoroughly combined.

Add the flour, bit by bit, mixing until everything is incorporated. Add the Daim pieces and mix to combine. Wrap the dough in clingfilm/plastic wrap and place in the refrigerator to chill for a few hours.

Preheat the oven to 190°C (375°F) Gas 5.

Form the dough into balls, each weighing about 40 g/1½ oz. and place on the prepared baking sheets 5 cm/2 in. apart. Bake in the preheated oven for 8–10 minutes until just golden. Remove from the oven and transfer to a wire rack – the middle should still be slightly soft but they will harden up.

rye & raisin cookies
cookies med rug & rosiner

150 g/1¼ sticks butter
150 g/1 cup plus 2 tablespoons plain/all-purpose flour
175 g/2⅛ cups rye flakes
½ teaspoon bicarbonate of/baking soda
1 teaspoon ground cinnamon
1 teaspoon ground mixed spice
½ teaspoon vanilla sugar
150 g/¾ cup caster/granulated sugar
100 g/½ cup dark molasses sugar
1 whole egg plus 1 egg yolk
2 tablespoons whole milk
150 g/1 cup raisins

baking sheet, greased and lined with baking parchment

MAKES 12 COOKIES

Melt the butter and set aside to cool. Combine the flour, rye flakes, bicarbonate of/baking soda and spices in a bowl and set aside.

Combine the sugars with the cooled, melted butter. Combine this with the egg, egg yolk and milk and mix with the flour mixture. Add the raisins and mix to combine. Wrap the dough in clingfilm/plastic wrap and place in the refrigerator to chill for a few hours.

Preheat the oven to 180°C (350°F) Gas 4.

Spoon out 12 cookies and place on the prepared baking sheet. Bake in the preheated oven for 8–10 minutes until only just done. Transfer to a wire rack and leave to cool before eating.

chocolate rye cookies
chokoladecookies med rugmel

150 g/1¼ sticks butter
200 g/1½ cups wholegrain rye flour
50 g/1¾ oz. cocoa powder
½ teaspoon bicarbonate of/baking soda
½ teaspoon vanilla sugar OR extract OR the seeds from 1 vanilla pod/bean
¼ teaspoon sea salt
150 g/¾ cup light brown soft sugar
100 g/½ cup caster/granulated sugar
1 wholel egg plus 1 egg yolk
2 tablespoons whole milk
100 g/⅔ cup milk/semisweet chocolate chips

2 baking sheets, greased and lined with baking parchment

MAKES 12 LARGE COOKIES

Melt the butter and set aside to cool. Combine the flour, cocoa, bicarbonate of/baking soda, vanilla and salt in a bowl and set aside.

Combine the sugars with the cooled, melted butter and stir until no lumps remain. Combine the egg, egg yolk and milk and mix with the sugar and butter until thoroughly combined.

Add the flour, bit by bit, mixing until everything is incorporated. Add the chocolate chips and mix to combine. Wrap the dough in clingfilm/plastic wrap and place in the refrigerator to chill for a few hours.

Preheat the oven to 190°C (375°F) Gas 5.

Form the dough into 12 balls and place on the baking sheets 5 cm/2 in. apart. Bake in the preheated oven for 8–10 minutes until just golden. Remove from the oven and transfer to a wire rack to cool – the middle will be slightly soft.

oat biscuits
havreflarn

180 g/1 cup minus 1½ tablespoons caster/granulated sugar
2 eggs
1 generous tablespoon plain/all-purpose flour
1 teaspoon baking powder
100 g/1 cup rolled oats
20 g/1½ tablespoons rye flakes (or plain rolled oats)
a pinch of salt
a drop of vanilla extract
50 g/3½ tablespoons butter, melted
50 g/1¾ oz. dark/bittersweet chocolate, melted

2 baking sheets, greased and lined with baking parchment

MAKES ABOUT 30

In a bowl, whisk the sugar and eggs until fluffy. In a separate bowl, sift together the flour and baking powder, then mix into the sugar and egg mixture with the oats, rye flakes (or extra oats), salt and vanilla. Stir together well. Pour in the melted butter, stirring until well combined. Leave at room temperature for 15 minutes before using.

Preheat the oven to 200°C (400°F) Gas 6.

Drop tablespoons of the mixture onto the prepared baking sheets, leaving at least 5 cm/2 in. between the biscuits as they will spread out a lot during baking.

Bake in the preheated oven for 5 minutes – the biscuits are done once they have a slight brown colour. Remove from oven, then transfer with a spatula to a cold surface to cool.

Decorate the biscuits with lines of melted chocolate. Leave to dry, then store in an airtight container.

rum treats
romkugler

These delicious treats were invented by the Danish bakers who needed a way to use up day-old Danish pastry and leftover bits of cake. Essentially, it is simply a few pastries, plus bits of cake and stuff to bind it together – mixed together and re-shaped. Most Danes living abroad will get a certain look in their eyes if you mention 'romkugler' – it's one of those things from back home that we really miss.

In Sweden, these are often known as Arraksbollar. To flavour, invest in a really good, strong rum extract or essence (can be bought online). If you don't have vermicelli strands, you can also roll in desiccated/dried shredded coconut or colourful sprinkles.

500 g/1 lb. 2 oz. leftover Danish pastries and/or cake – ideally a mixture of both
2–3 tablespoons good-quality raspberry jam/jelly
100 g/³⁄₄ cup minus ½ tablespoon icing/confectioners' sugar (add less if your cakes are a really sweet variety)
100 g/7 tablespoons softened butter
2 tablespoons cocoa powder
vanilla extract, to taste
2–3 teaspoons rum extract or essence (I use quite a concentrated one – you may need to add a bit more, as you want it to have a good punchy flavour)
a handful of oats (optional)
dark or light chocolate vermicelli strands, to decorate

MAKES 10–15

Roughly tear any Danish pastries into bite-sized pieces and crumble up any cakes you are using. In a stand mixer using the paddle attachment or in a food processor, blend the torn and crumbled pastries and cakes with the rest of the ingredients (apart from the oats and the chocolate vermicelli) until evenly mixed. Alternatively, you can do this by hand with a wooden spoon in a mixing bowl, but it will take longer.

Taste the mixture – it may need more cocoa powder, rum extract/essence or even icing/confectioners' sugar. Because this is made with leftovers, the taste will vary a bit. If you feel it needs more texture, you can add a handful of oats.

Chill the mixture in the refrigerator for about an hour to firm up.

Roll into balls a bit larger than the size of a golf ball and roll in the chocolate vermicelli strands to evenly coat. Chill again in the refrigerator until you are ready to serve.

Rum treats will keep well for 2–3 days wrapped in clingfilm/plastic wrap and stored in the refrigerator.

chocolate oat treats
havregrynskugler / chokladbollar

All Scandinavian kids know this basic chocolate treat recipe.
It requires no baking and is super-quick to make. In Sweden and
Norway, these are made all year round, but they're usually kept for
the festive season in Denmark. Make these ahead and keep them in
the fridge, as they last for a week or so. I tend to make a few batches
and flavour them for different tastes. Colourful sprinkles and gentle
flavours suit kids, but for a grown-up version, alcohol and more
coffee work well. Make a large quantity, split the mixture into several
batches and flavour each one at the end. I've included some favourite
variations below, but this recipe is perfect for experimentation.

250 g/2¼ sticks
   butter
400 g/scant 4 cups
   rolled oats
175 g/¾ cup plus
   2 tablespoons
   caster/
   granulated sugar
4 tablespoons
   cocoa powder
4 tablespoons
   strong, cooled
   coffee

1 teaspoon vanilla
   sugar
desiccated/dried
   shredded
   coconut, sugar
   sprinkles or
   pearl/nibbed
   sugar, to decorate

MAKES ABOUT 40

Blitz all the ingredients, except the coconut, sugar
sprinkles or pearl sugar in a food processor or mix by
hand (but allow the butter to soften before doing so).

Put the mixture in the fridge to firm up a bit before using
otherwise it can be a bit too sticky. Add more oats if you
feel the mixture is too soft.

Roll into 2.5-cm/1-in. diameter balls, then roll each ball
in desiccated/dried shredded coconut, sugar sprinkles
or pearl/nibbed sugar. Firm up in the fridge before eating
– they will keep in an airtight container for up to a week
in the fridge.

Variations
Orange – This one is for the grown-ups only. Add
2 tablespoons Cointreau and ¼ teaspoon orange zest
to 200 g/7 oz. of your mixture. Roll in chocolate sprinkles.

Almond – Another adults-only one. Add 2 tablespoons
Amaretto to 200 g/7 oz. of your mixture, then roll in
toasted, chopped almonds.

Raspberry– Children can enjoy this one. Add 1 tablespoon
raspberry jam/preserves to 200 g/7 oz. of your mixture.
Roll in freeze-dried raspberry pieces or sprinkles.

snowballs

snebolde

Marzipan features heavily in Nordic baking – and at Christmastime, even more so. We always use marzipan that has a high almond content – minimum 50% (the Danes prefer 63%, also known as raw marzipan). My kids love making these for the festive season (they often spray the snowballs with edible glitter, too).

200 g/7 oz. marzipan (63% almond content is the best for these sorts of treats, but you need at least a minimum of 50%)

120 g/4½ oz. good-quality white chocolate, roughly chopped

100 g/1⅓ cups desiccated/dried shredded coconut

cocktail sticks/ toothpicks
food-safe silver glitter (optional)

MAKES 20

Cut the marzipan into 20 pieces. Roll each piece into a ball, then leave to one side so they are cold when you add the chocolate – this allows them to dry quicker.

Temper the white chocolate. Melt half the chocolate in a very clean, dry, heatproof bowl set over a bain-marie until the chocolate is just liquid, then dab a little on the inside of your wrist – it should feel warm but not burning hot. Take the bowl off the bain-marie and quickly stir in the remaining chocolate. This will melt and bring down the temperature of the whole bowl and help to temper it.

Gently insert a cocktail stick/toothpick into a marzipan ball, then dip it in the melted chocolate so that it has a thin covering. Roll the ball in the desiccated/dried shredded coconut and leave to set on baking parchment.

Decorate with a little food-safe silver glitter, if you wish.

Variations
To flavour the marzipan, add a bit of grated orange zest when rolling the marzipan. For an adults-only version, adding 2 tablespoons Amaretto works well. For a more decadent version, roll the marzipan around small pieces of Viennese nougat.

vacuum cleaners
dammsugare

A cousin to the Danish Romkugler (see page 32), these treats from Sweden are also made using leftover cake and pastries. The name 'Vacuum Cleaners' is both because the shape looks a bit like a vacuum cleaner tube – and because, well, it was said to be made from all the bits the baker vacuumed up from the floor at the end of the day! Traditionally, the marzipan covering is green. For this, 25% marzipan is fine (this can be bought in normal supermarkets) – and you can colour it any shade you like to make a vibrant selection. In Denmark, these are often sold in bakeries two or three times the size of these. There, they are known as 'Tree Trunks' (Træstammer).

250 g/2½ cups crumbled leftover cake (store-bought Madeira, sponge, Swiss/jelly roll or similar)
75 g/¾ stick butter
1½ tablespoons cocoa powder
1 tablespoon raspberry jam/ preserve
rum essence or Ceylon Arrack liqueur, to taste
green food colouring paste
250 g/9 oz. marzipan or almond paste (at least 25% almond content) (see page 15)
icing/confectioners' sugar, to dust
150 g/5½ oz. dark/ bittersweet chocolate, melted

MAKES ABOUT 20

Put the cake crumbs, butter, cocoa, raspberry jam/ preserves and rum essence or arrack liqueur into a food mixer and mix on a medium setting until you have a smooth paste. Leave to rest in the fridge for an hour before rolling.

Meanwhile, add a few drops of green food colouring paste to the marzipan and work it with your hands until the colour is even.

Roll out the marzipan on a surface lightly dusted with icing/confectioners' sugar.

Roll out long logs of the cake mixture, approximately 1.5 cm/⅝ in. in diameter and lay one at a time on top of the marzipan. Roll enough of the marzipan around the cake mixture to cover completely and cut. Set aside seam-side down. Repeat until you have used all of the cake mixture and marzipan, then cut the logs into 6–7-cm/2½–2¾-in. pieces.

Dip each end of the logs in the melted chocolate and place on baking parchment. Leave to set in the fridge for 30 minutes before serving.

all the buns

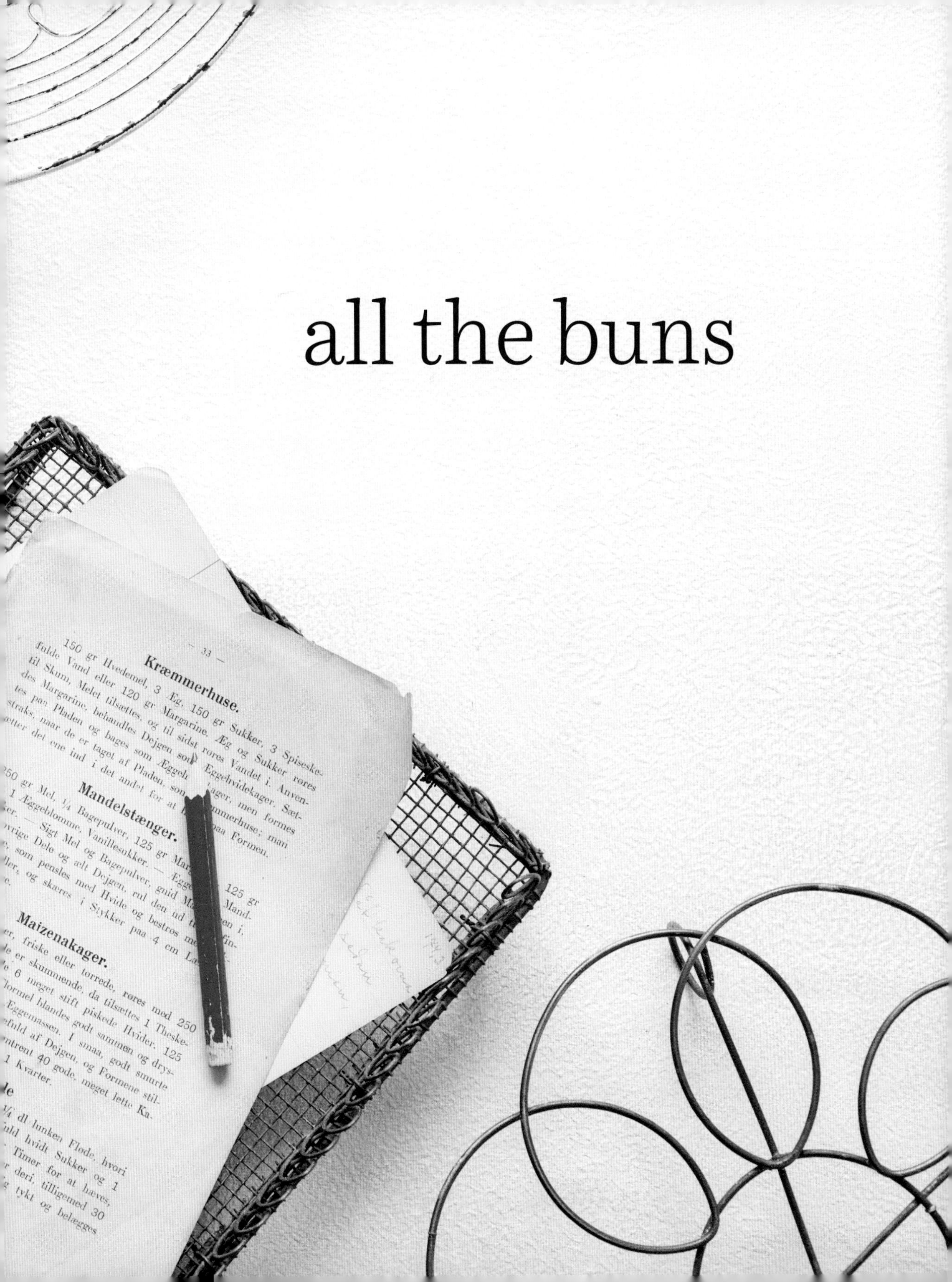

cinnamon share bake
kanellängd

Nothing says hygge and fika like a batch of fresh buns. I often make the entire batch as a wreath or sliceable share bake. In Sweden, the name Kanellängd means 'length of cinnamon' - in Danish, it's called Kanelstang. The Danish version usually has pastry cream and hazelnuts inside and is often finished with chocolate and plain white drizzle icing. In Sweden, pearl/nibbed sugar is added as decoration.

plain/all-purpose flour, for dusting
1 x quantity Basic Bun Dough (see page 52)
beaten egg, for brushing

REMONCE FILLING
100 g/1 stick minus 1 tablespoon softened butter
50 g/¼ cup dark brown soft sugar
50 g/¼ cup caster/granulated sugar
10 g/1½ tablespoons ground cinnamon
½ teaspoon vanilla extract
a pinch of salt

TO FINISH
100 g/3½ oz. min. 50% almond content marzipan, toasted nuts such as hazelnuts, or almonds (optional)
100 g/¾ cup minus ½ tablespoon icing/confectioners' sugar

2 baking sheets lined with baking parchment

MAKES 2 SHARING CINNAMON PASTRIES

SERVES 10–12 PEOPLE

Dust the work surface with flour and turn out the dough. Using a rolling pin, roll out the dough to a 50 x 25 cm/20 x 9¾ in. rectangle.

In a bowl, add all of the remonce filling ingredients and whisk together using an electric whisk until light and fluffy. Spread the filling over the rolled-out dough. Grate over the marzipan or sprinkle over the nuts, if using.

Roll up the dough lengthways into a long, tight roll. Using a sharp knife, cut in half widthways into two long pieces. Put one roll on each prepared baking sheet. Using a pair of scissors, cut all the way along almost to the base, but not quite, of the roll at around 1 cm/½ in. intervals. Flip the cinnamon rolls to alternate sides all the way down, then flatten slightly. This will create a plait/braid-like pattern. Leave to rise for 20–25 minutes.

Preheat the oven to 200°C (400°F) Gas 6.

Brush each plait/braid with egg and bake in the preheated oven for around 20–25 minutes or until baked through. Overbaked means dry, so do check it. If the top is getting too brown but the middle is not baked, you can add foil to the top while it finishes – as well as turn the heat lower. Remove from the oven and leave to cool.

Mix the icing/confectioners' sugar with a little hot water until you have a consistency of treacle, then add to a piping/pastry bag fitted with a small plain nozzle/tip and pipe over each pastry. Serve in slices.

real cinnamon buns
kanelbullar

Your cinnamon buns will taste different to mine, just like
my mother's taste different to her mum's and different to my
neighbour's - and everyone else. Cinnamon buns are personal
because you knead the love into them. Everybody makes them their
own way, even if they don't realise. This is a basic recipe for
cinnamon buns. Try it - then go make them yours and make them
for people you love. Trust me, after 3-4 batches, you will know what
I mean: the recipe will become yours, and yours alone.

plain/all-purpose
  flour, for dusting
1 x quantity Basic
  Bun Dough (see
  page 52)
beaten egg, for
  brushing

FILLING
80 g/¾ stick
  butter, at room
  temperature
1 teaspoon plain/
  all-purpose flour
1 tablespoon
  ground
  cinnamon
½ teaspoon ground
  cardamom
½ teaspoon vanilla
  sugar
80 g/⅓ cup plus
  1 tablespoon
  caster/
  granulated sugar

SYRUP
3 tablespoons
  golden syrup/
  light corn syrup
  and 6
  tablespoons
  water, heated
  in a saucepan

TOPPING
pearl/nibbed sugar
  or chopped,
  toasted nuts

*2 baking sheets,
  greased and lined
  with baking
  parchment*

MAKES 16

Dust the work surface with flour and turn out the
bun dough. Knead the dough with your hands and work
in more flour if needed. Using a rolling pin, roll out the
dough to a 40 x 50 cm/16 x 20 in. rectangle.

For the filling, in a bowl, add the butter, flour, spices and
sugars and mix together well. Using a spatula, spread
the mixture evenly over the rolled-out dough. Carefully
roll up the dough lengthways into a long roll. Using
a sharp knife, cut into 16 even slices.

Put the swirls onto the prepared baking sheets (not
too close as they will rise further). Leave to prove under
a dish towel for 30 minutes.

Preheat the oven to 200°C (400°F) Gas 6.

Brush each bun lightly with beaten egg and pop the
buns into the preheated oven to bake for around 10–12
minutes. Watch the buns as they bake: they can go dark
very quickly and you may also need to move the buns
around in the oven if they are not baking evenly.

When golden, remove from the oven. Brush the buns
lightly with the warmed syrup then decorate with the
pearl/nibbed sugar or chopped, toasted nuts.
Immediately place a damp, clean dish towel on top for
a few minutes to prevent the buns from going dry.

apple & cinnamon buns
bullar med äpple och kanel

My kids love apple and cinnamon and these make a lovely afternoon treat as an alternative to the usual buns.

3 eating apples, peeled, cored and chopped into 5 mm/¼ in. pieces

2 tablespoons ground cinnamon

60 g/5 tablespoons caster/granulated sugar

1 teaspoon cornflour/cornstarch

1 x quantity Basic Bun Dough (see page 52)

plain/all-purpose flour, for dusting

leftover pastry cream and/or leftover marzipan pieces (optional)

egg, for brushing

icing/confectioners' sugar, for dusting

a baking sheet, lined with baking parchment

MAKES 16

Preheat the oven to 180°C (350°F) Gas 4.

Put the apple pieces into a large bowl. Sprinkle over the cinnamon, sugar and cornflour/cornstarch and set aside.

Dust the work surface with flour and turn out the bun dough. Knead the dough with your hands and work in more flour if needed. Divide the dough into 16 equal buns. Roll each bun well and add to the prepared baking sheet – and press them down flat (they will rise again, but for now, give them a firm push down).

Leave to rise for about 15 minutes, then press down again in the middle to make a deep indent around 4 cm/1½ in. in diameter. Spoon in some pastry cream or marzipan (if using) and then add a good spoonful of apples.

Leave again for another 10 minutes, brush the sides with the beaten egg and then bake in the preheated oven until done – around 10–15 minutes.

Leave to cool down then dust with icing/confectioners' sugar before serving.

semlor buns

semlor

Lent is celebrated across Scandinavia. The Swedish semlor buns, traditionally eaten on Mardi Gras, are made from a yeast dough. Filled with marzipan paste and cream, these really do make for a treat.

plain/all-purpose flour, for dusting
1 x quantity Basic Bun Dough (see page 52) adding 1 teaspoon baking powder with the dry ingredients

FILLING
100 g/3½ oz. marzipan (see page 15)
good dollop of custard or Pastry Cream (see page 14)

500 ml/2 cups whipping cream
1 teaspoon vanilla sugar
icing/confectioners' sugar, to dust

piping/pastry bag fitted with a plain nozzle/tip

MAKES 12

Turn the dough out onto a floured surface. Knead again for a few minutes, adding more flour if needed. You want a firmer but not dry dough. Cut the dough into 12 equal-sized pieces and shape each into a ball. Place, evenly spaced, on a baking sheet. Leave to rise for 25–30 minutes.

Preheat the oven to 200°C (400°F) Gas 6.

Brush each bun with the remaining beaten egg and bake for 8–10 minutes or until baked through – keep an eye on them as they can burn quickly. Remove from the oven and cover the buns with a lightly damp dish towel immediately to prevent them from forming a crust.

When they have cooled completely, cut a 'lid' off the buns – about 15 mm/½ in. from the top. Scoop out about one-third of the inside of each bun and place this in a separate bowl. Mix it with the marzipan/almond paste until it forms a very sticky mass – add a dollop of custard or pastry cream at this point to help it along. You want a spoonable, even mixture. Spoon the filling back into the buns, equally divided.

Whip the cream with the vanilla sugar until stiff, then use the piping/pastry bag to pipe cream on all the buns. Put the 'lids' back on and dust lightly with icing/confectioners' sugar. Serve.

Variation
Lemon – Fill the hole with 1 tablespoon of store bought lemon curd and add lemon zest to the top.

birthday buns
fødselsdagsboller

Grandma Inger used to make these for our birthdays when we were kids, and she'd let us put so much butter on them that our teeth made an indent with every bite (this is known as tandsmør in Danish – literally, toothbutter – such a great word!). Now I bake these for my own kids – but always with a thought to Inger in her warm kitchen, always busy doing something but never too busy to hug us and play with us kids. She was an amazing person and I miss her always.

200 ml/¾ cup whole milk

50 ml/3½ tablespoons single/light cream

25 g/1 oz. fresh yeast or 13 g/2½ teaspoons dried/active/dry yeast

50 g/¼ cup caster/granulated sugar

400 g/3 cups strong white/bread flour, plus extra for dusting

1 teaspoon salt

1 egg

80 g/¾ stick butter, softened

beaten egg, for brushing

a baking sheet, greased and lined with baking parchment

MAKES 12

Mix together the milk and cream and heat to finger-warm (around 36–37°C/97–98°F).

If using fresh yeast, add the yeast and warmed milk-cream to a stand mixer with a dough hook attached. Mix until the yeast has dissolved.

If using dried/active dry yeast, pour the warmed milk and cream into a bowl. Sprinkle on the yeast and whisk together. Cover with clingfilm/plastic wrap and leave in a warm place for about 15 minutes to activate and become frothy. Pour into the stand mixer with a dough hook.

Add the sugar and stir again, slowly adding half the flour mixed with the salt. Add the egg and softened butter and keep mixing. Slowly add the other half of the flour. You may not need all the flour or you may need a bit more, but keep mixing until you have a slightly sticky dough that is starting to let go of the sides of the bowl. This should take around 5–7 minutes.

Cover the bowl with clingfilm/plastic wrap and leave to rise for around 35–40 minutes or until doubled in size.

Turn the dough out onto a lightly floured surface and knead through with your hands, adding only a little more flour if needed. Cut the dough into 12 equal pieces and roll them into round balls. Place on the prepared baking sheet. Cover again and leave to rise for a further 20 minutes.

Preheat the oven to 200°C (400°F) Gas 6.

Brush each bun lightly with beaten egg, then bake in the preheated oven for 10–12 minutes or until golden brown.

Remove from the oven and place a damp, clean dish towel on top for a few minutes if you prefer the buns without a hard crust. Serve sliced open, with butter or some Scandinavian sliced cheese.

basic bun dough

13 g/2½ teaspoons dried/dry active yeast
   or 25 g/1 oz. fresh yeast *(see below)
250 ml/1 cup plus 1 tablespoon whole milk,
   heated to 36–37°C (97–99°F)
80 g/¾ stick butter, melted and left to
   cool slightly
40 g/3¼ tablespoons caster/granulated sugar
400–500 g/3–3²/₃ cups strong white/bread flour
2 teaspoons ground cardamom
1 teaspoon salt
1 egg, beaten
flaked/slivered almonds, to decorate

MAKES ABOUT 16

Pour the warm milk into a bowl, sprinkle in the
yeast and whisk together. Cover with clingfilm/
plastic wrap and leave in a warm place for about
15 minutes to become bubbly. Pour into the bowl
of a food mixer fitted with a dough hook. Start the
machine and add the cooled, melted butter. Allow
to combine with the yeast for 1 minute or so, then
add the sugar. Allow to combine for 1 minute.
In a separate bowl, weigh out 400 g/3 cups of the
flour, add the cardamom and salt and mix together.
Start adding the flour and spices into the milk
mixture, bit by bit. Add half the beaten egg. Keep
kneading for 5 minutes. You may need to add more
flour – you want the mixture to end up a bit sticky,
but not so much that it sticks to your finger if you
poke it. It is better not to add too much flour as this
will result in dry buns. You can add more later. Once
mixed, leave the dough in a bowl and cover with a
dish towel or clingfilm/plastic wrap. Leave to rise for
around 30 minutes or until it has doubled in size.

*If using fresh yeast, add the warm milk to a small
bowl and crumble in the yeast; stir until dissolved,
then pour into the bowl of the mixer.

tosca buns
toscabullar

1 x quantity Basic Bun Dough (see left)
1 quantity Vanilla Filling (see page opposite)
50 g/½ cup chopped almonds
salt flakes, to sprinkle (optional)

TOSCA TOPPING
100 g/1 stick minus 1 tablespoon butter,
   at room temperature
100 g/1¼ cups flaked/slivered almonds
80 g/⅓ cup plus 1 tablespoon dark brown
   soft sugar
2 tablespoons plain/all-purpose flour
50 ml/3½ tablespoons double/heavy cream

*2 baking sheets, greased and lined
   with baking parchment*

MAKES ABOUT 16

Boil the tosca topping ingredients together
in a saucepan for 1 minute until thickened. Leave
to cool. Turn the dough out onto a lightly floured
surface and knead through, working in more flour
if needed. Roll out the dough to a 40 x 50 cm/16
x 20 in. rectangle. Spread the vanilla filling evenly
all over using a spatula. Scatter over the chopped
almonds. Carefully roll up the dough lengthways
into a long, tight roll. Using a sharp knife, cut into
16 even slices and put onto the prepared baking
sheets. Leave to rise in a warm place for a further
20 minutes under a clean kitchen cloth.
Preheat the oven to 200°C (400°F) Gas 6.

Brush each bun lightly with the reserved beaten
egg (from the dough) and spoon a good amount
of tosca topping over each bun. Scatter with salt
flakes (if using) and bake in the preheated oven
for 10–12 minutes until golden. Remove from the
oven and leave to cool a little before serving.

blueberry buns
blåbärbullar

1 x quantity Basic Bun Dough (see page opposite)
150 g/5½ oz. frozen blueberries
simple sugar syrup, for brushing (see right)

VANILLA FILLING
80 g/¾ stick butter, at room temperature
1 tablespoons plain/all-purpose flour
1 teaspoon vanilla sugar or extract,
   or seeds from 1 pod/bean
100 g/½ cup caster/granulated sugar

_2 baking sheets, greased and lined with baking
   parchment_

MAKES ABOUT 24

Turn the dough out onto a lightly floured surface
and knead, working in more flour if needed. Roll out
the dough to a 40 x 50 cm/16 x 20 in. rectangle.
Mix together the filling ingredients and spread
evenly over the dough. Scatter the dough with one
third of the blueberries. Fold one third of the dough
on top of the other side of the dough and then fold
the remaining dough on top of this, so you get a
three-layer parcel; around 45–50 x 12–15 cm/18–20
x 5–6 in. Cut the dough into about 16 strips. Hold
one end of a strip with a floured hand, then twist
the loose end of the dough. Once it starts to
entwine on itself, twist the whole strip into a knot,
ensuring that the end is tucked underneath. Put on
the baking sheets and repeat with the remaining
strips. Press the rest of the blueberries into the folds.

Preheat the oven to 180°C (350°F) Gas 4.

Leave to rise in a warm place for a further 20
minutes under a kitchen cloth, then brush with the
reserved beaten egg. Bake in the preheated oven
for 7–9 minutes until golden. Brush lightly with
sugar syrup before serving.

rhubarb buns
rabarberbullar

1 x quantity Basic Bun Dough (see page opposite)
¼ quantity of Pastry Cream (see page 14)
2–3 rhubarb sticks, chopped into 3-cm/1¼-in. pieces
caster/granulated sugar, for sprinkling and rolling
simple sugar syrup, for brushing (1 part white sugar:
   1 part water – boiled, then used warm)

_2 baking sheets, greased and lined with baking
   parchment_

MAKES ABOUT 16

Turn the dough out onto a lightly floured
surface and knead through, working in more flour
if needed. Cut into 16 equal pieces, then roll each
one into a uniformly round shape and space out
on the prepared baking sheets. Cover with a clean
kitchen cloth and leave in a warm place to rise
for about 10 minutes.

Take a glass or an object with a similar cylindrical
shape of approx. 3 cm/1¼ in. wide and dip the
end in flour. Press indents in all the buns. Fill each
indent with a tablespoon of pastry cream and top
with 2–3 pieces of rhubarb.

Preheat the oven to 180°C (350°F) Gas 4.

Leave to rise for a further 15–20 minutes, then
brush with the reserved beaten egg (from making
the dough) around the edges. Sprinkle a little
sugar on the rhubarb.

Bake the buns in the preheated oven for about
8 minutes until cooked through and golden. Remove from the oven and brush the sides with the
warm sugar syrup. Roll the sides in sugar to coat –
a bit like a doughnut.

marzipan choux buns

kartoffelkager

The name of these Danish éclairs translates as 'potato cakes', but there are no hidden potatoes in them. The name stems from their look, not the ingredients.

CHOUX BUNS

170 g/scant 1¼ cups strong white/ bread flour

½ teaspoon salt

¼ teaspoon baker's ammonia (see page 11; these will still work without, it just makes the pastry extra crisp)

125 g/1⅛ sticks butter

1 tablespoon caster/ granulated sugar

4–5 eggs, mixed together and placed in a small jug/pitcher

FILLING

250 ml/1 cup plus 1 tablespoon whipping cream

¼ quantity Pastry Cream (see page 14)

TOPPING

300–400 g/10 ½–14 oz. store-bought marzipan with 50% almond content (or see basic Marzipan recipe on page 15)

icing/confectioners' sugar and cocoa powder, for dusting

a large piping/ pastry bag fitted with large plain nozzle/tip (optional)

2 baking sheets, greased and lined with baking parchment

a 5-cm/2-in. round pastry/cookie cutter

MAKES 25

Preheat the oven to 200°C (400°C) Gas 6.

Sift together the flour, salt and baker's ammonia (if using). Put the butter and sugar into a saucepan with 275 ml/scant 1¼ cups of water and melt together over a low heat. Add the flour and stir until incorporated and the mixture lets go of the sides of the pan. Remove from the heat and leave to cool for a few minutes.

Add the eggs, a little at a time, to the cooled dough, beating well between each addition. You may not need all the eggs. You want to end up with a smooth mixture that still holds if piped, but drops from the spoon in about 3–4 seconds.

Spoon or pipe out around 25 buns of equal generous size onto the prepared baking sheets, spaced well apart. Put in the preheated oven and immediately reduce the heat to 180°C (350°F) Gas 4. Bake for 20–25 minutes until well risen and golden brown. Try not to open the oven door during the baking time. To make sure the buns are cooked, take one out and see if it collapses. If it sinks, bake the buns for a few more minutes. Remove from the oven and poke a small hole in each bun to let the steam escape. Leave to cool down completely on a wire rack.

No more than 2 hours before serving, whip the cream to stiff peaks, then fold in the pastry cream. Cut each bun open and pipe in a generous amount of filling to taste.

Roll out the marzipan on a surface lightly dusted with icing/confectioners' sugar. Stamp out shapes to fit over the tops of the choux pastry buns using the round cutter. Add the marzipan circles to the top and dust with cocoa.

norwegian cream buns
skoleboller

Every Norwegian will know of this bun. Literally translated, the name skoleboller means 'school buns' because these buns are often added to packed lunches or sold at bake sales. I do prefer making these with pastry cream – but, if you choose to use a custard, you need to heat and thicken it a bit with cornflour/cornstarch otherwise it will spread too much when baking (and make sure your well in the bun is deep).

plain/all-purpose flour, for dusting
1 x quantity Basic Bun Dough (see page 52)
½ x quantity Pastry Cream (see page 14)
150 g/1 cup icing/confectioners' sugar
100 g/1⅓ cups desiccated/dried shredded coconut
½ beaten egg, for brushing

a baking sheet lined with baking parchment

MAKES 12 LARGE BUNS

Preheat the oven to 180°C (350°F) Gas 4.

Dust the work surface with flour and turn out the dough. Knead the dough with your hands and work in more flour if needed. Cut the dough into 12 equal-sized pieces. Roll out so the buns are uniform in size and shape and place on the prepared baking sheet, well spaced out.

Leave for about 10 minutes to rest, then prod a large hole in the middle of each one and flatten slightly – so you end up with a hole around 4 cm/1½ in. in diameter. Add a large tablespoon of the pastry cream to each one. Leave for another 15 minutes to rise, then brush the sides of the buns with the beaten egg.

Bake in the preheated oven for around 10–12 minutes or until done and golden along the sides.

When the buns have cooled slightly, make the icing by mixing the icing/confectioners' sugar with a little hot water until you have a syrup-like consistency. Carefully – I use a pastry brush for this – brush the icing around the edges of the buns, then scatter the coconut on top (try not to get too much on top of the custard, the coconut is just for the edges). Leave to set before serving.

Variation

In Sweden, the same bun is known as Vaniljbullar (Vanilla Buns). There, instead of the icing and coconut, the just-out-of-oven buns are brushed with a bit of melted butter and dipped in caster/granulated sugar.

gingerbread buns

pepparkaksbullar

When Christmas comes around, I like to flavour my cinnamon
buns with a more festive filling – so I add pepparkakskryddor –
gingerbread spices – to my bun filling. I think these are super-festive.

plain/all-purpose
  flour, for dusting
1 x quantity Basic
  Bun Dough
  (see page 52)
beaten egg, for
  brushing
100 ml/⅓ cup plus
  1 tablespoon
  golden syrup/
  light corn syrup
pearl/nibbed sugar,
  to decorate
  (optional)
icing/confectioners'
  sugar, to dust

FILLING
120 g/1⅛ sticks
  soft butter
50 g/¼ cup caster/
  granulated sugar
50 g/¼ cup light
  brown sugar
1–2 tablespoons
  gingerbread
  spice mix;
  depending on
  how spiced you
  like it, ready
  mixed or make
  your own
  (see right)

**GINGERBREAD SPICE
MIX (YIELDS ABOUT
2 TABLESPOONS)**
2 teaspoons ground
  cinnamon
2 teaspoons ground
  ginger
1 teaspoon ground
  cloves
1 teaspoon ground
  cardamom
½ teaspoon ground
  allspice

*a baking sheet,
  greased and lined
  with baking
  parchment*

**MAKES 14–15 SMALL
BUNS**

Dust the work surface with flour and turn out the
dough. Knead the dough with your hands and work in
more flour if needed. Using a rolling pin, Using a rolling
pin, roll out the dough to a 40 x 50 cm/16 x 20 in.
rectangle.

For the filling, cream all the ingredients together in
a bowl until smooth. Spread the filling across the dough
in an even, thin layer.

To make traditional swirls, simply roll up the dough
lengthways into a long roll and cut into 15 slices, place
on the prepared baking sheet, cover with a kitchen towel
and leave to rise for a further 20 minutes.

To make the knots, fold the prepared dough in half and
cut into strips. Take a strip and hold down one edge with
your finger and use your hand to roll the strip in on itself,
as tight as it will go, then arrange into a neat circle,
taking care that both ends are tucked away underneath
otherwise they will unfold when baking.

Meanwhile, preheat the oven to 200°C (400°C) Gas 6.

Brush the buns lightly with the beaten egg, then bake
in the preheated oven for 9–10 minutes or until golden
and done. Watch them carefully, they can burn easily.

Meanwhile, melt the syrup in a saucepan. When the buns
come out of the oven, immediately brush lightly with
the syrup, then add pearl/nibbed sugar (if using) on top
of the buns and cover with a damp kitchen towel. Just
before serving, sprinkle with icing/confectioners' sugar.

chocolate buns
chokladbullar

Adding chocolate to buns is a great way to give them a makeover. However, just adding chocolate chips doesn't really do it – you need a spread or more liquid filling. Store-bought hazelnut spread is a great way of adding chocolate to the buns.

1 x quantity Basic Bun Dough (see page 52)

FILLING

50 g/3½ tablespoons butter, softened

75 g/⅓ cup plus 2 teaspoons light brown soft sugar

4 large heaped tablespoons chocolate hazelnut spread (such as Nutella)

1 tablespoon plain/all-purpose flour, plus extra for dusting

50 g/2 oz. good-quality milk/semisweet chocolate, chopped (I use Lindt or Marabou)

beaten egg, for brushing

2–3 tablespoons golden/light corn or date syrup

a generous handful of toasted hazelnuts, roughly chopped

a baking pan with sides, greased and lined with baking parchment

MAKES 16

For the filling, in a food processor or stand mixer, combine the butter, sugar, chocolate hazelnut spread and flour and blend until you have a smooth, spreadable mixture. Set aside.

Dust the work surface with flour and turn out the dough. Knead the dough with your hands and work in more flour if needed. Using a rolling pin, roll the dough out to a large rectangle of around 30 x 40 cm/11¾ x 16 inches.

Spread the chocolate filling in an even layer across the dough. Scatter with the chopped chocolate.

Roll the dough up tightly lengthways to form a long sausage, then cut into 16 even pieces using a knife or pizza cutter.

Squash the buns tightly together into the prepared baking pan if you would prefer a traybake to tear and share (pictured). Or if you want to make individual buns then space them evenly on two larger lined baking sheets. Cover with a clean kitchen cloth and leave to rise for a further 20 minutes.

Preheat the oven to 200°C (400°F) Gas 6.

Brush the buns with a little beaten egg, then bake in the preheated oven for around 8–10 minutes or until golden brown. Remove the buns from the oven, then brush immediately with the golden/light corn or date syrup. Decorate each bun with toasted chopped hazelnuts. Immediately place a damp, clean kitchen cloth on top for a few minutes to prevent the buns from going dry.

everyday cakes & pies

60 Kv. Maribo Dampmølles Flormel, blandet med ½
Bagepulver, ½ Thekop tynd Fløde og tilsidst 8 pi-
skede Hvider. Bages ¾ Time.

213

Det kokta riset upplägges lätt i ring på ett fat,
och äpplena läggas så hela som möjligt i mitten.
Sockerlagen hälles över. Kan serveras med 1 kkp
vispad grädde (eller god mjölk).
   Samma rätt kan uppläggas varvtals med ris och
frukt i en skål. Uppvispad grädde hälles då över.

253

Apelsin med ris.

1 kkp risgryn
1 liter vatten
apelsiner, 1 citron

¾ kkp socker
2 kkpr tjock grädde
(4 blad gelatin)

Risgrynen sköljas och påsättas i kokande vatten
sakta koka, tills gröten är tjock.
Då riset är kallt, nedblandas det riv...
...ronen, sockret jämte saften av a...

...atinet lägges i kal...
...nsmaken ...

banana rye bread
bananbrød

Banana bread isn't a big thing in Scandinavia, but it's a bestseller at my café. We came up with a recipe that contains wholegrain rye flour, which gives the final product a lovely nutty flavour and takes it from feeling a bit like a cake to more of a bread. I toast my banana bread lightly and add cinnamon butter – it's a perfect morning treat.

4 very ripe bananas
100 g/scant ½ cup Greek yogurt
1 tablespoon freshly squeezed lemon juice
1 teaspoon vanilla extract or vanilla sugar
125 g/1 cup minus 1 tablespoon plain/all-purpose flour
125 g/1 generous cup wholemeal/wholewheat rye flour
½ teaspoon salt
1 teaspoon bicarbonate of/baking soda

125 g/1⅛ sticks butter, softened
150 g/¾ cup dark brown soft sugar
2 UK large/US extra-large eggs
cinnamon butter (see below right), to serve (optional)

a 500-g/1-lb. loaf pan, greased and lined with baking parchment

MAKES 1 LOAF

Preheat the oven to 180°C (350°F) Gas 4.

Peel and mash the bananas and mix with the yogurt, lemon juice and vanilla and set aside.

Mix the flours with the salt and bicarbonate of/baking soda and set aside.

Cream together the butter and dark brown soft sugar in a stand mixer fitted with the paddle attachment, or using a hand-held electric whisk. Add the eggs, one at a time, scraping down the sides of the bowl between each addition to ensure they are fully incorporated.

Add the mashed banana mixture and mix until incorporated, then add the flours and mix briefly until smooth. Do not over-mix.

Spoon the mixture evenly into the lined loaf pan. Bake in the middle of the preheated oven for around 30 minutes, or until a skewer inserted into the middle comes out just clean. Leave to cool a little before turning out of the pan onto a wire rack. Cut into slices and serve toasted, with plenty of cinnamon butter (see below).

CINNAMON BUTTER
Mix 3 tablespoons of strong cinnamon sugar (ratio 1:3) with half a packet of softened butter – re-chill and use as needed.

mazarin cake
mazarintærte

This is a super-quick one-mix cake. Traditionally, it is made with store-bought marzipan, but I have adapted it slightly as 50% marzipan is hard to get hold of in some places. It's a simple cake – it doesn't need much adding to it. Never serve this warm, it is much nicer cold, which allows for the almond flavour to really come through. You can add a variety of toppings to this cake, but I like it with the melted chocolate topping. Sometimes, simple really is best.

200 g/2 cups ground almonds
150 g/³⁄₄ cup caster/sugar
150 g/1 cup icing/confectioners' sugar
150 g/1¼ sticks butter, softened
2 teaspoons almond extract
1 teaspoon vanilla extract
4 eggs
100 g/³⁄₄ cup plain/all-purpose flour
50 g/½ cup cornflour/cornstarch
a pinch of salt
2 teaspoons baking powder

TOPPING
150 g/5½ oz. chocolate of your choice (I prefer dark/bittersweet but you can mix it)
150 ml/²⁄₃ cup double/heavy cream

a 23-cm/9-in. round baking pan, greased and lined with baking parchment

SERVES 10–12

Preheat the oven to 175°C (350°F) Gas 4.

In a food processor, whizz the ground almonds (to make them even finer), then add the sugars and whizz again. Add the butter and extracts (if it's still too thick, add a dash of cold water, too). Next, add the eggs, one by one. Combine the flour, cornflour/cornstarch, salt and baking powder and mix in (do not over-mix once the flour is added).

Pour into the prepared baking pan and bake in the preheated oven for around 35–40 minutes, or until a skewer inserted in the centre comes out clean. Cool completely in the pan before turning out onto a serving plate.

When the cake has cooled, melt the chocolate and cream together for the topping. Spread over the top and sides of the cake and leave to set. Serve cold.

Variations
Omit the chocolate topping, leave the cake to cool completely then top with freshly whipped cream and fresh berries.

Sometimes, in Sweden, this cake is served with a simple icing as a topping instead of chocolate.

easy lemon & blueberry bundt
nem citron & blåbærkage

When I was a child, I used to come home from school, throw my bag on the floor and head straight to the kitchen to make an 'After School Cake', basically, a cake that a child could bake, and quickly! My kids often come home and want to bake, too, but starting a big project an hour before dinner isn't quite doable. This recipe is based on a 'Sockerkaka' base - a sugar cake, in Swedish. You can top it with anything. from berries to nuts, and flavour with anything from cardamom to vanilla.

30 g/¹⁄₃ cup
   breadcrumbs
325 g/1¹⁄₂ cups plus
   2 tablespoons
   caster/
   granulated sugar
4 eggs
1 teaspoon vanilla
   extract
300 g/2¹⁄₄ cups
   plain/all-purpose
   flour
2 teaspoons baking
   powder
¹⁄₂ teaspoon salt
50 g/3¹⁄₂
   tablespoons
   butter, melted
100 ml/¹⁄₃ cup plus
   1 tablespoon
   whole milk
zest and juice
   of 1 large lemon

50 g/¹⁄₄ cup
   Greek yogurt
100–150 g/
   3¹⁄₂–5¹⁄₂ oz.
   blueberries or
   bilberries
icing/confectioners'
   sugar, for dusting
whipped cream,
   to serve

a 25-cm/9³⁄₄-in.
   bundt or ring pan,
   greased with
   butter

SERVES 10

Preheat the oven to 180°C (350°F) Gas 4.

Dust the prepared bundt or ring pan with breadcrumbs, then tip out the excess.

In a mixing bowl, whisk the sugar, eggs and vanilla extract until thick, light and fluffy using a balloon or hand-held electric whisk. Mix the remaining dry ingredients together and sift into the egg mixture. Fold in until incorporated.

Add the melted butter, milk, lemon zest and juice and yogurt and fold gently until completely combined.

Pour the batter into the prepared pan. Add the blueberries or bilberries – they'll sink quite a bit during baking. Bake in the preheated oven for 30–35 minutes or until a skewer inserted in the centre comes out clean. Cool completely in the pan before turning out onto a serving plate. Dust with icing/confectioners' sugar and serve with whipped cream.

Variations
Grated orange zest and fresh raspberries is a delicious combination – or vary with lime zest, too.

banana muffins
bananmuffins

My daughter, Astrid, and I have done our best to ruin this basic muffin recipe by chopping and changing the ingredients and have made many, many versions in our kitchen. As long as you follow the recipe for the quantities of fats and sugars, you should be okay.

250 g/1¾ cups plus 2 tablespoons plain/
   all-purpose flour
120 g/½ cup plus 1½ tablespoons light brown sugar
2 teaspoons baking powder
½ teaspoon salt
2 eggs
100 g/scant ½ cup natural/plain yogurt
100 ml/⅓ cup plus 1 tablespoon neutral oil

FILLING
1 teaspoon vanilla extract
1 teaspoon ground cinnamon
1 banana, peeled and chopped
5–10 strawberries, chopped (depending on size)

a muffin pan lined with non stick muffin cases

MAKES APPROX. 12

Preheat the oven to 180°C (350°F) Gas 4.

Add the dry ingredients to a bowl and mix. Add the wet ingredients and mix 8–10 times with a wooden spoon or spatula until incorporated (do not overmix). Add the filling ingredients and mix until just combined. Spoon into the muffin cases, taking care not to over-fill them. Bake in the preheated oven for 15–20 minutes (depending on your filling, this can vary – a smaller muffin needs a shorter bake) and bake until done (when a skewer inserted comes out clean). Remove from the pan and transfer to a wire rack to cool down.

chocolate muffins
chocolademuffins

Try adding either white or milk chocolate chips to this mixture.

250 g/1¾ cups plus 2 tablespoons plain/
   all-purpose flour
50 g/½ cup cocoa powder
120 g/½ cup plus 1½ tablespoons light brown
   sugar
2 teaspoons baking powder
½ teaspoon salt
2 eggs
100 g/scant ½ cup natural/plain yogurt
100 ml/⅓ cup plus 1 tablespoon neutral oil

FILLING
1 teaspoon vanilla extract
a handful of milk chocolate chips
a dash of milk

a muffin pan lined with non stick muffin cases

MAKES APPROX. 12

Preheat the oven to 180°C (350°F) Gas 4.

Add the dry ingredients to a bowl and mix. Add the wet ingredients and mix 8–10 times with a wooden spoon or spatula until incorporated (do not overmix). Add the filling ingredients and mix until just combined. Spoon into the muffin cases, taking care not to over-fill them.

Bake in the preheated oven for 20–25 minutes (depending on your filling, this can vary – a smaller muffin needs a shorter bake) and bake until done (when a skewer inserted comes out clean). Remove from the pan and transfer to a wire rack to cool down.

mango & peanut butter muffins
mangomuffins med jordnød

Simply because this is a surprisingly good combination.

250 g/1¾ cups plus 2 tablespoons plain/all-purpose flour
120 g/½ cup plus 1¼ tablespoons light brown sugar
2 teaspoons baking powder
½ teaspoon of salt
2 eggs
100 g/scant ½ cup natural/plain yogurt
100 ml/⅓ cup plus 1 tablespoon neutral oil

FILLING
1 teaspoon vanilla extract
100 g/3½ oz. chopped fresh mango pieces
100 g/3½ oz. crunchy peanut butter
a handful of chopped peanuts (optional)

a muffin pan lined with non stick muffin cases

MAKES APPROX. 12

Preheat the oven to 180°C (350°F) Gas 4.

Add the dry ingredients to a bowl and mix. Add the wet ingredients and mix 8–10 times with a wooden spoon or spatula until incorporated (do not overmix). Add the filling ingredients and mix until just combined. Spoon into the muffin cases, taking care not to over-fill them.

Bake in the preheated oven for 20–25 minutes (depending on your filling, this can vary – a smaller muffin needs a shorter bake) and bake until done (when a skewer inserted comes out clean). Remove from the pan and transfer to a wire rack to cool down.

vegan blueberry muffins
vegansk blåbærmuffin

Replace eggs in muffins by adding banana.

250 g/1¾ cups plus 2 tablespoons spelt flour
120 g/½ cup plus 1½ tablespoons light brown sugar
2 teaspoons baking powder
½ teaspoon salt
2 mashed ripe bananas
100 g/scant ½ cup soy yogurt or similar
100 ml/⅓ cup plus 1 tablespoon neutral oil

FILLING
1 teaspoon vanilla extract
1 teaspoon ground cardamom
1 teaspoon xanthan powder
a handful of blueberries or other berries to your liking (frozen berries work well)
a handful of oats, to top before baking

a muffin pan lined with non stick muffin cases

MAKES APPROX. 12

Preheat the oven to 180°C (350°F) Gas 4.
Add the dry ingredients to a bowl and mix. Add the wet ingredients and mix 8–10 times with a wooden spoon or spatula until incorporated (do not overmix). Add the filling ingredients and mix until just combined. Spoon into the muffin cases, taking care not to over-fill them. Sprinkle with the oats.

Bake in the preheated oven for 20–25 minutes (depending on your filling, this can vary – a smaller muffin needs a shorter bake) and bake until done (when a skewer inserted comes out clean). Remove from the pan and transfer to a wire rack to cool down.

daim tart
daimtårta

While this cake is not perhaps traditional, it does hold a place in the food hearts of many as a cake one can buy when visiting that Swedish place with all the flat-packed furniture! It doesn't contain any flour, so is naturally free from gluten.

200 g/1½ cups whole almonds, skin on
160 g/1 cup plus 2 tablespoons icing/confectioners' sugar
5 egg whites
a pinch of salt

TOPPING
5 egg yolks
100 ml/⅓ cup plus 1 tablespoon whipping cream
100 g/½ cup caster/granulated sugar
150 g/1¼ sticks butter, cut into small pieces, at room temperature

CHOCOLATE COVERING
100 g/3½ oz. good-quality milk/semisweet chocolate, roughly chopped
100 ml/⅓ cup plus 1 tablespoon double/heavy cream
4 Daim bars, chopped

2 x 23-cm/9-in. round cake pans, greased and lined with baking parchment

SERVES 6–8

Preheat the oven to 160°C (325°F) Gas 3.

In a food processor, grind half of the almonds and pulse until fine, then add the rest and pulse so that you have a mixture of fine and semi-rough. Add the icing/confectioners' sugar and pulse together again.

In a stand mixer, whisk the egg whites with a pinch of salt until stiff peaks form (not more). Add the ground almond mixture and gently fold in until incorporated.

Pour the mixture into the prepared cake pans and bake in the preheated oven for 35–40 minutes or until light brown and a skewer inserted into the middle comes out clean. Turn out carefully onto a wire rack and leave to cool completely. Baking time can vary, so do watch it.

Meanwhile, make the topping. Put the egg yolks, whipping cream and caster/granulated sugar into a saucepan over a low heat. Bring just to the boil, whisking constantly – as soon as you see the first bubble, quickly take the pan off the heat or the yolks will cook. To check the mixture is thick enough, dip a spoon in it, then run your finger through the back of the spoon; if the line stays, the mixture is ready. Leave the mixture to cool to room temperature. Slowly beat in the butter using a hand-held electric whisk, a little at a time, until you have a thick, glossy topping. If it's too runny, put it in the fridge to set then whisk again.

Spread ⅔ of the topping mixture onto the first almond base, add the top layer of almond cake and spread the remaining topping on the top and over the sides.

Place in the fridge for an hour for the topping to harden up. Melt the chocolate with the double/heavy cream over a bain-marie and spread across the top and sides, then sprinkle the Daim pieces on top of the still warm chocolate and leave to set in the fridge. Serve cold.

swedish sticky cake
kladdkaka

Kladd means sticky in Swedish, and this cake has to be under-baked to be good. The original recipe only contains cocoa powder – and if it is over-baked it becomes dry. Your oven will be different to mine, so do experiment with the baking time. A good rule of thumb is to take the cake out two minutes before you think you should; the edges should be just-baked and the top starting to form a crust. It might still be sticky in the centre, which is okay as it will continue baking in the pan. The original recipe calls for milk or dark chocolate, but I love the gooey white chocolate version, too.

150 g/1¼ sticks butter
150 g/5½ oz. good-quality white chocolate (or milk/semi-sweet or dark/bittersweet chocolate), broken into pieces
2 eggs
200 g/1 cup caster/granulated sugar
150 g/1 cup plus 2 tablespoons plain/all-purpose flour or cake flour
a pinch of salt
2 teaspoons vanilla sugar OR extract OR use the seeds from 1 vanilla pod/bean
½ teaspoon grated lemon zest
optional toppings (see method)

a 23-cm/9-in. springform/springclip round cake pan, greased and lined with baking parchment

SERVES 6–8

Preheat the oven to 180°C (350°F) Gas 4.

Melt the butter in a saucepan over a low heat. Remove from the heat and stir in the white chocolate pieces until melted. Set aside.

Beat together the eggs and caster/granulated sugar until pale and fluffy in a stand mixer or using a hand-held electric whisk. Sift the dry ingredients into a separate bowl and fold gently into the egg and sugar mixture. Fold in the lemon zest and chocolate-butter until combined.

Pour into the prepared cake pan and place in the preheated oven immediately. Bake for 15–17 minutes until the cake is just under-baked. The middle should still be really sticky and only the side should be fully baked. Keep an eye on it, as baking times will vary. If it wobbles, it still needs a little more time in the oven. A skewer inserted 2 cm/¾ in. from the edge should come out clean.

Leave the cake to cool in the pan for at least an hour before transferring to a serving plate. If you think you have overbaked it, then remove from the pan immediately to stop the baking process. Serve the kladdkaka on its own or with one of the toppings below:

Double chocolate: Finely chop 50 g/2 oz. of your favourite chocolate and mix with whipped cream and ½ teaspoon cocoa powder. Works with milk/semisweet or dark/bittersweet chocolate kladdkaka.

Mixed berries: Top with fresh redcurrants and blueberries and dust with icing/confectioners' sugar. Serve with whipped cream. Works with all types of kladdkaka.

Variation
For milk/semisweet chocolate kladdkaka, omit the lemon zest and add 2 tablespoons golden/light corn syrup and extend the cooking time slightly.

rhubarb cake
rabarberkage

When I was expecting my youngest daughter I had a bit of an addiction to pastry cream. We also had an abundance of rhubarb that year and I had so much to use in every way I could think of. This cake is the result of expecting Elsa (I made about five other versions with different berries and fruit, too – but all full of pastry cream!).

175 g/1½ sticks butter, softened
200 g/1 cup caster/granulated sugar
4 eggs, lightly beaten
200 g/1½ cups plain/all-purpose flour or cake flour
1 teaspoon vanilla sugar OR extract OR use the seeds from 1 vanilla pod/bean
½ teaspoon salt
1½ teaspoons baking powder
150–200 g/5½–7 oz./¾–1 cup Pastry Cream (see page 14)

TOPPING
400 g/14 oz. rhubarb
30 g/¼ stick butter
50 g/¼ cup caster/granulated sugar
2 teaspoons ground cardamom

a 23-cm/9-in. springform/springclip round cake pan, greased and lined with baking parchment

SERVES 8

Preheat the oven to 180°C (350°F) Gas 4.

First, make the topping. Wash the rhubarb and chop into 2 cm/¾ in. pieces. In a saucepan set over a low heat, melt the butter, then stir in the caster/granulated sugar and ground cardamom. Add the chopped rhubarb, stir to coat in the butter and stew for 2–3 minutes to start the cooking process, then remove from the heat and set aside to infuse.

To make the cake, cream together the butter and sugar in a stand mixer with a whisk attachment (or using a hand-held electric whisk) until pale and fluffy. Add the eggs to the mixture, bit by bit, whisking constantly but stopping to scrape down the sides of the bowl if necessary. Ensure all the egg is fully incorporated before adding more.

Combine the dry ingredients and sift into the egg mixture. Fold in until incorporated. Pour the batter into the prepared cake pan and spread out evenly. Spread the pastry cream evenly on top of the batter.

Remove the rhubarb from the syrup and scatter over the cake. Reserve the syrup for drizzling over the cake later.

Bake in the preheated oven for 1 hour (lowering the heat if the top gets too dark). A skewer indserted into the middle of the cake should come out clean, however, the pastry cream will remain a bit wet. Remove from the pan and allow to cool slightly before drizzling with the leftover rhubarb syrup and cutting into slices to serve.

love cake

kärleksmums

This cake has many, many names across Scandinavia. We call it Love Cake (from the Swedish 'kärlek', meaning 'love', and 'mums' meaning something delicious). In Denmark, it is known as 'Den du ved nok', which roughly translates as 'That cake, you know...' - and thus, it has no other name! I make it using a more devil's food cake base to keep it nice and moist. The topping is so good I can just eat it by the spoonful on its own.

50 g/½ cup good-quality cacao powder
100 ml/⅓ cup plus 1 tablespoon very hot water
100 ml/⅓ cup plus 1 tablespoon whole milk
200 g/1¾ sticks butter, softened
225 g/1 cup plus 2 tablespoons caster/granulated sugar
3 eggs
225 g/1¾ cups plain/all-purpose flour
½ teaspoon salt
1 teaspoon vanilla sugar
1 teaspoon bicarbonate of/baking soda

TOPPING
150 g/1 cup icing/confectioners' sugar
50 g/3½ tablespoons butter
1 large tablespoon cacao powder
½ teaspoon vanilla sugar
4 tablespoons filter coffee
50 g/¾ cup desiccated/dried shredded coconut, plus extra to decorate
sea salt flakes (optional)

a 20 x 20-cm/8 x 8-in. cake pan, greased and lined with baking parchment

SERVES 9

Preheat the oven to 180°C (350°F) Gas 4.

Mix together the cacao powder and hot water and leave to cool a bit. Add the milk to the cacao mixture.

Cream the butter and sugar until pale. Add the eggs, one by one, taking care they are completely incorporated.

In a bowl, sift together the flour, salt, vanilla sugar and bicarbonate of/baking soda.

Add the flour and the cacao mixture to the egg mixture whilst whisking continuously on a medium setting, taking care to ensure everything is well incorporated – but do not overmix or you will end up with a heavy cake.

Pour the batter into the prepared cake pan and bake in the middle of the preheated oven for 20–25 minutes or until a skewer inserted comes out just clean (take care not to overbake). When the cake is done, cool slightly in the pan then transfer to a wire rack and leave to cool completely.

To make the topping, combine all the ingredients in a saucepan over a low heat and let melt and combine. Spread over the cooled cake and top with extra coconut and a few sea salt flakes. Leave to set before serving.

ginger cakes
krydderkage/pepparkaka

These cakes are easy to make and they smell like Christmas!
The batter makes a standard 30 x 25 cm/11¾ x 9¾ in. cake or loaf
pan – or several individual loaves as pictured here. This recipe
can also be used to make a gingerbread layer cake – split the batter
between two round springform/springclip pans and assemble with
a vanilla buttercream. If you don't have access to lingonberries,
you can leave them out or use raspberries.

175 g/1½ sticks
   butter
3 eggs
150 g/¾ cup caster/
   granulated sugar
100 g/½ cup light
   brown soft sugar
300 g/2¼ cups
   plain/all-purpose
   flour
2 teaspoons baking
   powder
2 teaspoons ground
   cinnamon
1 teaspoon ground
   ginger
1 teaspoon ground
   cloves
1 teaspoon ground
   cardamom
a pinch of salt
½ teaspoon vanilla
   extract
220 ml/scant 1 cup
   whole milk

100 g/3½ oz. frozen
   lingonberries

ICING
150 g/1 cup icing/
   confectioners'
   sugar
pink food colouring
decorations, such
   as sugar rose
   petals or
   sprinkles

*14 mini rectangular
   cake pans
   (4 x 10-cm/
   1½ x 4-in. each)
   or a large loaf
   pan, greased and
   lined with baking
   parchment*

SERVES 14

Preheat the oven to 180°C (350°F) Gas 4.

Melt the butter and set aside to cool a little.

Using a balloon whisk or a hand-held electric whisk,
whisk the eggs with the caster/granulated and light
brown soft sugar in a bowl until light and fluffy.

Combine the dry ingredients in a separate bowl, then sift
into the egg mixture and fold in gently. Add the melted,
cooled butter, vanilla extract and milk and fold again
until incorporated.

Divide the mixture between the prepared loaf pans or
transfer to the large cake pan and add the berries on top.

Bake in the preheated oven for around 15 minutes
or until well-risen, golden brown and springy to the
touch. Baking time depends on the pans you use – you
can make this as a big cake and cut out in pieces, then
decorate – or bake in individual moulds. A skewer
inserted into the middle should come out clean. Turn
the cakes out onto a wire rack and leave to cool.

To make the icing, add a little hot water to the icing/
confectioners' sugar along with a few drops of pink food
colouring. You want a thick, treacle-like mixture. Carefully
add the icing to the top of the cooled cakes and then
decorate as you wish.

danish dream cake
drømmekage

This cake is one of the first I learned to bake. To this day, I still absolutely love the coconut topping – it really makes the simple base stand out. The origin of this cake is from a 1950s baking competition in Denmark where a young girl entered this cake and won (it was her grandmother's recipe). It is one of the most loved cakes in Denmark.

3 eggs
225 g/1 cup plus 2 tablespoons caster/granulated sugar
½ teaspoon vanilla sugar
225 g/1¾ cups plain/all-purpose flour or cake flour
2 teaspoons baking powder
150 ml/⅔ cup whole milk
75 g/¾ stick butter, melted

TOPPING
100 g/1 stick minus 1 tablespoon butter
150 g/2 cups desiccated/dried shredded coconut
250 g/1¼ cups dark brown sugar
75 ml/⅓ cup whole milk
a pinch of salt

a 23-cm/9-in. springform/springclip or round cake pan, greased and lined with baking parchment

SERVES 10–12

Preheat the oven to 190°C (375°F) Gas 5.

In the bowl of a food mixer, whisk the eggs, caster/granulated sugar and vanilla sugar on a high speed for a few minutes, until white and light. Meanwhile, in a separate bowl, sift the flour and baking powder together.

Carefully fold the flour into the egg mixture. Mix the milk with the melted butter in a jug/pitcher and carefully pour into the batter, folding it in until incorporated. Pour the batter into the prepared cake pan.

Bake in the preheated oven for 35–40 minutes, or until almost done (try not to open the oven door for the first 20 minutes of the total baking time).

Meanwhile, to make the topping, put all the ingredients in a saucepan and gently melt together.

Remove the cake from the oven and carefully spread the topping all over the cake. Return to the oven. Turn up the heat to 200°C (400°F) Gas 6 and bake for a further 5 minutes.

Leave the cake to cool in the pan before eating, if you can (we are well aware it's hard to do that!).

hazelnut & strawberry mousse cake
jordbærmousse med hasselnøddebund

This cake has origins in an old Danish Easter recipe – but, more recently, a similar cake was made famous by a Danish bakery chain. I've baked this for many fika get-togethers and varied the berries in the mousse, but nothing beats strawberries when they are in season.

HAZELNUT CAKE LAYER
200 g/1½ cups toasted hazelnuts
4 egg whites
150 g/¾ cup caster/granulated sugar
2 tablespoons good-quality cocoa powder
1 teaspoon vanilla extract or sugar

STRAWBERRY MOUSSE
4 gelatine sheets
300 ml/1½ cups whipping cream
1 teaspoon vanilla extract or sugar

400 g/14 oz. strawberries
50 g/¼ cup caster/superfine sugar
mixed berries, to decorate
edible rose petals, to decorate

a 22-cm/8¾-in. round cake pan, greased and lined with baking parchment

SERVES 6

Preheat the oven to 180°C (350°F) Gas 4.

In a food processor, grind half of the toasted hazelnuts and pulse until well ground. Chop the remaining hazelnuts into small pieces.

Whisk the egg whites until light foam peaks form, then add the sugar, cocoa powder and vanilla and fold until smooth. Fold in all the hazelnuts. Pour into the prepared cake pan. Bake in the preheated oven until done – depending on your oven, this can take 25–35 minutes. Remove from the oven and leave to cool.

Soften the gelatine leaves in cold water for approx. 10 minutes. Put the whipping cream and vanilla into a large bowl and whip until stiff. Set aside in the fridge.

Meanwhile, blend the strawberries in a blender until smooth. Pass through a sieve/strainer – you should end up with around 350 g/12 oz. strawberry purée. Put the sugar and purée in a saucepan over a low heat.

Squeeze the gelatine leaves to remove any excess water, then add to the warm strawberry mixture. Whisk to combine. Remove from the heat and leave to cool.

Add ¼ of the cold whipped cream to the strawberry purée and mix well, then pour the strawberry mix into the remaining cream and fold carefully. It is important the mixture is not hot. Pour into a bowl or piping bag and leave to chill for at least 2 hours or, ideally, overnight. To assemble, put the hazelnut base on a plate, pipe the mousse on top and finish with berries and edible petals.

scandi custard tarts
linser

The first mention of this cake was in a Danish cookbook from 1648. It hasn't changed much: the sweet shortcrust pastry in a round shape, filled with pastry cream and then baked with a top until just baked through – but not so long that the pastry cream seeps out. I think this could be considered to be the Scandinavian version of a custard tart – every country seems to have one! I love adding raspberry jam/preserves to these, but the original recipe is just plain pastry cream. Make sure your pastry cream is made with real vanilla for great depth of flavour.

plain/all-purpose flour, for dusting
1 x quantity Sweet Shortcrust Pastry (see page 14) (chilled)
approx. 150 g/ 5½ oz. good-quality raspberry jam/preserves
1 x quantity Pastry Cream (see page 14) (cold)
icing/confectioners' sugar, to serve

15–20 muffin cases
2 x 12-cup muffin pans
7-cm/2¾-in. and 6-cm/2⅓-in. round cutters

MAKES 15–20 TARTS

Preheat the oven to 180°C (350°F) Gas 4.

Dust the work surface with flour and roll out the pastry to approx. 3 mm/⅛ in. thick. Cut circles with the larger cutter and line the muffin cases with the pastry rounds. Add a small teaspoon of jam/preserves to each of the pastry bases, then add enough pastry cream to fill almost to the top (leave a little space).

Roll out the remaining pastry and use the smaller cutter to cut out the tops. Place one on top of each tart and press each circle down gently around the edge to close the tart completely.

Put the muffin pans into the preheated oven and bake for 15–16 minutes until baked through. Be careful, if it gets too hot the custard will expand and start to escape.

Remove from the oven and leave to cool completely in the pans before removing the tarts from the cases.

Serve these tarts cold with a light dusting of icing/confectioners' sugar.

Variations
I sometimes make these with cloudberry jam instead – it's delicious. My kids love a bit of Nutella in the base – or simply leave plain for the more traditional version.

bilberry & cardamom pie
blåbärtårta

During the long Nordic summers, we go bilberry picking. Bilberry is a wild blueberry - the colour is deep and intense all the way through the berry. It turns everything a deep purple. In Scandinavia we simply call them blåbär (blueberries) - and we often get a little surprised when we eat blueberries elsewhere as they don't have the same intensity that we're used to. If you can't get hold of bilberries, use blueberries - frozen are absolutely fine. The result will be a little less liquid, but still delicious.

plain/all-purpose flour, for dusting
½ x quantity Sweet Short Crust Pastry (see page 14)
200–300 g/ 7–10½ oz. frozen bilberries (or blueberries)
1–2 tablespoons cornflour/ cornstarch or a grated eating apple (depending on how juicy your berries are)
1 teaspoon ground cardamom
½ teaspoon grated orange zest
¼ x quantity Pastry Cream (see page 14) (optional)

MAZARIN BASE
150 g/5½ oz. 50% almond content marzipan
75 g/6 tablespoons caster/ granulated sugar
100 g/1 stick minus 1 tablespoon butter, softened
2 eggs
50 g/heaping ⅓ cup plain/ all-purpose flour
pinch of salt

a 28-cm/11-in. round tart pan (loose-bottomed is great – but you can also line with baking parchment and use a closed pan or dish)

SERVES 8

Preheat the oven to 180°C (350°F) Gas 4.

To make the mazarin base, in a stand mixer with the paddle attachment, beat the marzipan and the sugar until well combined, then add the butter and the eggs, one by one. Sift in the flour and salt and fold gently into the egg mixture.

Dust the work surface with flour and roll out the pastry until you have a piece that fits your pan and also goes well over the edges (you may have some left over). Transfer to the prepared pan.

Add the bilberries to a bowl and then add the cornflour/ cornstarch (or apple) and cardamom and orange zest (you can use other citrus fruit if you prefer).

Spoon the marzipan mixture into the pastry case. If you're adding the pastry cream, gently add a little on top of the marzipan. Add the bilberries on top (if you find these are too wet, drain before adding – blueberries will usually not contain as much juice as bilberries).

Bake the pie in the preheated oven for about 40 minutes or until it is baked through. Leave to stand in the pan for several hours before slicing.

mamma lena's apple pie
mor's æbletærte

Baking is very personal. My mum makes an apple pie that takes me back to my childhood in one bite. I think it is utterly wonderful how we can time travel when we eat certain things, even if it's only for one split second. My mum is a warm, wonderful person - and even as an adult, her hugs are what make me feel safer in a confusing world.

6–7 Granny Smith apples (don't use cooking apples for this – only eating apples; Granny Smith is best, but a similar sour note apple can also be used)

50 g/¼ cup dark brown sugar

50 g/¼ cup caster/granulated sugar

1 teaspoon vanilla sugar

15 g/½ oz. ground cinnamon

1 heaped teaspoon cornflour/cornstarch

a pinch of salt

1 x quantity Sweet Short Crust Pastry (see page 14)

plain/all-purpose flour, for dusting

beaten egg, for brushing

1 teaspoon caster/granulated sugar, for sprinkling

a 28-cm/11-in. round tart pan (loose bottomed is great – but you can also line with baking parchment and use a closed pan or dish)

SERVES 8

Preheat the oven to 180°C (350°F) Gas 4.

Peel and core the apples and slice. I like to keep my slices not too thick – around 5 mm/¼ in. a slice.

Weigh out the sugars, cinnamon and cornflour/cornstarch and make sure they are well mixed. Add to a large plastic food bag and add the apples. Toss to coat.

Split the pastry into two portions ⅔ and ⅓.

Lightly flour the work surface and roll out the large piece of pastry until you have a piece that fits your pan and also goes well over the edges. Transfer to your lined pan.

Add the thoroughly coated apples to the pastry case – up to you if you want to arrange them nicely or just throw them all in there.

Roll out the top from the remaining pastry piece and cover the top of the pie completely, pressing the edges to seal. Cut a few pie vents with a knife and then brush the top with beaten egg. Scatter a little caster/granulated sugar on top.

Bake in the preheated oven for around 40–45 minutes or until it is baked through and the apples are soft. Leave to stand in the tart pan for 15–30 minutes before slicing.

You may need to turn down the heat after 15 minutes baking if the pie is getting too much colour on top – turn to 160°C (325°F) Gas 3 and bake for a little longer. Note – there may be a bit of dough left over – you can freeze this and use at a later date.

traybakes
& rolled cakes

179

250 g Margarine, 125 g Kartoffelmel, 125

...men med Melis; Margarinen tilsættes,
...s Melet i, Hviderne piskes og kom-
... og bager en knap Time.

...100 g Mel, lidt Salt).
...efter tilsættes Melet
...igen hviler nu ½
...med et Vin-
...arm Ovn.
Sukker

rye & raspberry brownie

rugmelsbrownie med hindbær

Like most of the things I bake at home, I like my brownie recipe
to be adaptable to suit whatever ingredients I have in the cupboard.
If this means I can get away with adding a bit more fibre, then all the
better! This brownie is made only with wholegrain rye flour, which
gives it a lovely nutty undertone.

250 g/1 cup plus
2 tablespoons
butter
100 g/3½ oz. good
quality dark/
bittersweet
chocolate
100 g/3½ oz.
good-quality
milk/semisweet
chocolate
275 g/1½ cups
minus 2
tablespoons
caster/
granulated sugar
3 eggs
75 g/½ cup plus 1
tablespoon
wholemeal rye
flour

50 g/½ cup
good-quality
cocoa powder
(I use Fazer
kakao)
1 teaspoon baking
powder
a pinch of salt
1 teaspoon vanilla
sugar or extract
150 g/5½ oz.
raspberries

a 28 x 20-cm/
11 x 8-in. brownie
pan, greased and
lined with baking
parchment

MAKES 9–12

Preheat the oven to 180°C (350°F) Gas 4.

Melt the butter and chocolates in a heatproof bowl
set over a pan of barely simmering water. Do not let the
base of the bowl touch the water. Alternatively, you can
melt the chocolates in the microwave, but take care
to just melt, don't cook them. Set aside to cool.

Whisk together the caster/granulated sugar and eggs by
hand using a balloon whisk in a large mixing bowl. There
is no need to whisk in loads of air as you don't want the
brownie to rise too much. Ensure the melted chocolate-
butter has cooled, then stir into the sugar-egg mixture.

Sift the flour, cocoa powder, baking powder, salt and
vanilla sugar into the bowl and fold into the mixture
with a spatula until smooth. Take care not to overwork
the mixture. Fold in half of the raspberries. Pour the
mixture into the prepared brownie pan. Add the rest
of the raspberries on top and press down lightly.

Bake in the preheated oven for 25–30 minutes or until
a skewer inserted into the side comes out clean – the
middle can still be gooey (but it should not wobble when
you shake the pan). Leave to cool in the pan then cut into
squares to serve.

Note: Baking times will vary. Brownies are quite
forgiving if you cook them on a lower heat for a longer
time – so keep checking the edges and just make sure
you don't overbake it. It's nicer with a slightly
underbaked brownie rather than being overbaked.

rye flapjacks
mueslibar

Most people have a go-to flapjack or cereal bar recipe. I love making mine with honey – and I think that date syrup always adds depth of flavour. I make these for my kids' lunch boxes as their treat. It's a very forgiving recipe – I make these with what I have in the cupboard. The secret to a flapjack success is to know when to remove it from the oven, depending on your preference for crumbly or gooey – and also packing it down firmly before baking. If you don't have dates, use something else – nuts, seeds, other dried fruit – just keep the quantity to around 150 g/5½ oz. in total.

200 g/¾ cup plus 2 tablespoons butter
50 ml/3 tablespoons runny honey
100 g/½ cup light brown soft sugar
pinch of salt
75 ml/5 tablespoons date syrup
250 g/2½ cups rolled oats
100 g/⅔ cup rye flakes
75 g/½ cup raisins
75 g/½ cup chopped dates

a 30 x 20-cm/ 11¾ x 8-in. baking pan, greased and lined with baking parchment

MAKES 12

Preheat the oven to 160°C (325°F) Gas 3.

Put the butter, honey, sugar, salt and date syrup into a saucepan. Heat gently until just melted and hot. Add the oats, rye flakes and dried fruit and stir.

Spoon the mixture into the prepared pan and press down very firmly so no air pockets remain.

Bake in the preheated oven for around 25 minutes – but keep an eye on it. The longer you bake, the crispier the result, so if you like your flapjack extra-chewy, take it out a little earlier.

Mark where the slices will be on the hot flapjack using a knife, then leave to cool completely in the pan before turning out and cutting into slices.

The flapjacks will keep for up to a week stored in an airtight container.

raspberry squares
hindbærsnitter

As a child growing up in Denmark, these raspberry squares were a favoured treat from the local bakery on the walk home from school, if I had a few coins in my pocket. It's a very simple treat – and kids (not least mine) love the sweet shortcrust pastry mixed with a good jam, some icing and lots of sprinkles.

1 x quantity Sweet
  Shortcrust Pastry
  (see page 14)
200 g/½ cup
  good-quality
  raspberry jam/
  jelly
300 g/2 cups plus 2
  tablespoons
  icing/
  confectioners'
  sugar

1–3 tablespoons
  hot water
sprinkles,
  to decorate

*2 baking
  sheets, greased
  and lined with
  baking
  parchment*

MAKES 12–16

Preheat the oven to 180°C (350°F) Gas 4.

Split the sweet shortcrust pastry into two equal portions and roll into two evenly-sized squares, around 3 mm/ ⅛ in. thick. Each one should be around 30 x 30 cm/ 11¾ x 11¾ in. Ensure the shapes are the same size as you will be layering them later.

Put the pastry squares on the prepared baking sheets. Prick the surfaces with a fork to prevent air bubbles forming as they bake. Pop in the preheated oven to bake for about 10–12 minutes or until slightly golden. Remove from the oven and set aside to cool on a wire rack.

On one of the cooled pastry sheets, spread a generous, even layer of the raspberry jam/jelly. Very carefully, slide the other piece of pastry on top so that it sits exactly on top of the base. Handle delicately, as the pastry can break quite easily.

Mix the icing/confectioners' sugar with hot water to form a smooth paste. The amount of water you will need varies depending on your sugar. If the paste is too thick, add a few drops more water. Too thin, add a bit more icing/confectioners' sugar. Aim for the consistency of runny honey. Spread the icing on top of the pastry to evenly cover. Top with sprinkles and leave to dry.

Using a very sharp knife, cut the edges off the pastry to make straight sides. Cut into small equal pieces to serve.

easy chocolate roll
chokladrulltårta

Versatility and simple recipes is the key when I bake at home. This chocolate Swiss roll bakes quickly and you can adapt the filling to suit your mood. A walnut and cream filling is simple and delicious, but you can replace the nuts with raspberries and you have an entirely different cake. Replace the cocoa with plain/all-purpose flour for a vanilla roll.

4 eggs
120 g/²/₃ cup minus 1 teaspoon caster/superfine sugar
90 g/²/₃ cup plain/all-purpose flour
30 g/¹/₃ cup cocoa powder, plus extra for dusting
½ teaspoon baking powder
a pinch of salt
1 teaspoon vanilla sugar or extract
25 g/1³/₄ tablespoons butter, melted and cooled
50 g/2 oz. dark/bittersweet chocolate, for the topping

FILLING
300 ml/1¹/₄ cups whipping cream
brandy or walnut liqueur (optional)
75 g/³/₄ cup toasted walnut pieces, chopped

a Swiss roll/jelly roll pan, approx. 30 x 20-cm/11³/₄ x 8-in., greased and lined with baking parchment

SERVES 6–7

Preheat the oven to 180°C (350°F) Gas 4.

In the bowl of a stand mixer, add the eggs and the sugar and whisk until they reach the ribbon stage (this may take several minutes on full speed). It's done when you can see ribbon traces on the surface when lifting the whisk from the bowl.

Mix the flour, cocoa powder, baking powder, salt and vanilla sugar together, then sift into the egg mixture and fold gently until combined. Add the melted butter and fold in, being careful not to knock the air out.

Pour the mixture into the prepared pan. Bake in the preheated oven until just baked through – the time will depend on your oven, but it is around 10–12 minutes. It is done when it is slightly springy to the touch.

Remove from the oven and allow to cool for a few minutes. Cover the pan with a clean dish towel, then turn the cake out onto the dish towel. Carefully remove the paper backing. Gently roll the log around the tea towel/dish towel while it is still warm – this should prevent the roll from cracking later when filled. Leave to cool completely on a wire rack.

Meanwhile, for the filling, whip the cream to form stiff peaks. When the roll has cooled, unroll carefully and brush with the brandy or walnut liqueur, if using. Add the whipped cream in a thin, even layer and top with the chopped walnuts. Carefully roll it back around the filling and place on a serving tray.

Dust the whole roll with cocoa powder. Melt the chocolate in a bain-marie or microwave. Add to a piping/pastry bag and snip the end off, then pipe the chocolate all across the roll and serve.

kvæfjord cake
kvæfjordkake

This cake is often described by Norwegians as the 'world's best cake', which is quite a statement. This cake contains the most delicious whipped cream, sponge, pastry cream and meringue – it's everything you could ever want wrapped up together in one bite. This cake is so seriously good that it is also often labelled the 'national cake of Norway'.

150 g/1¼ sticks butter, softened
130 g/⅔ cup caster/granulated sugar
5 egg yolks
150 g/1 cup plus 2 tablespoons plain/all-purpose flour or cake flour
1 teaspoon baking powder
1 teaspoon vanilla sugar OR extract OR use the seeds from 1 vanilla pod/bean
100 ml/⅓ cup plus 1 tablespoon whole milk

FILLING
150 ml/⅔ cup whipping cream
½ x quantity Pastry Cream (see page 14)

MERINGUE TOPPING
5 egg whites
a pinch of cream of tartar
250 g/1¼ cups caster/granulated sugar
75 g/⅔ cup flaked/slivered almonds

a 25 x 35-cm/9¾ x 14-in. rectangular cake pan, greased and lined with baking parchment

SERVES 8–10

Preheat the oven to 160°C (325°F) Gas 3.

In a stand mixer (or using a hand-held electric whisk), cream together the butter and sugar until pale and light. Add the egg yolks, one at a time, beating to ensure everything is well incorporated. Sift in the plain/all-purpose or cake flour, baking powder and vanilla sugar and fold in. Lastly, add the whole milk and fold again until fully combined. Spoon the mixture into the prepared pan and spread out evenly, then set aside for a moment.

Next, make the meringue topping. Using a clean bowl, whisk the egg whites with the cream of tartar until soft peaks form. Add the sugar very slowly, bit by bit, beating on a high speed until stiff peaks form (about 5 minutes). Spread the meringue mixture on top of the cake mixture. Scatter the flaked/slivered almonds on top.

Bake in the preheated oven for 35–40 minutes or until a skewer inserted into the middle comes out clean and the meringue is firm. Leave to cool for a few minutes in the pan, then turn out carefully, so the meringue is still on top. Leave to cool completely on a wire rack.

For the filling, whip the cream until stiff peaks form and then fold together with the pastry cream.

To assemble, cut the cake into two halves. On one half, spread the pastry cream mixture, then carefully layer the other cake half on top. Leave to set in the refrigerator for an hour before serving. The meringue will stay mallowy and the base soft. Cut into slices to serve.

vegan chocolate & nut cake
vegansk chokoladekage

This cake is based on an old recipe, from when eggs, milk and butter were often in short supply. There are countless types of recipes online, and a lot stem from the Depression era and the Second World War. Sometimes these cakes are known as 'wacky cakes' or 'war cakes', but there are many different versions – how people made do with what was available at the time, I just don't know. This is not my base recipe, but I have adapted it to my liking by adding things to keep the cake moist and to bake properly (but still reducing the oil content a bit to avoid an oily aftertaste). Some vegan cakes today follow similar principles when baking of using a vinegar reaction to replace the need for eggs.

40 g/1½ oz. good-quality dairy-free cocoa powder
250 ml/1 cup plus 1 tablespoon boiling water
1 teaspoon vanilla sugar or extract
180 g/1⅓ cups plain/all-purpose flour
180 g/1 cup minus 1½ tablespoons caster/granulated sugar
½ teaspoon salt
1 teaspoon bicarbonate of/baking soda
1 teaspoon baking powder
1 tablespoon apple cider vinegar

2 large heaped tablespoons store-bought apple sauce (not too sweet)
60 ml/¼ cup neutral-tasting oil
100 g/3½ oz. mixed, lightly chopped nuts (pistachio nuts, walnuts, hazelnuts and/or almond mix)
sea salt flakes

a 28 x 20-cm/ 11 x 8-in. brownie pan, greased and lined with baking parchment

SERVES 5–6

Preheat the oven to 180°C (350°F) Gas 4.

Put the cocoa powder into a bowl and add the water, just off the boil, and mix. Leave to cool a little.

In a separate bowl, add all of the dry ingredients and mix together.

Add the apple cider vinegar to the cocoa and mix together, then add to the dry mixture. Add the apple sauce and oil and mix until smooth (do not overmix).

Pour the mixture into the prepared brownie pan. Scatter the nuts over the top and a sprinkle of salt flakes. Bake in the preheated oven for 20–24 minutes until a skewer inserted in the centre comes out clean. Let cool. Slice and serve.

Tip: If you want a more chocolatey cake, add 50 g/1¾ oz. melted dark/bittersweet 70% dairy-free chocolate to the mixture. You can also add an icing made from 50 g/1¾ oz. melted 70% dairy-free chocolate, 100–150 g/¾–1 cup icing/confectioners' sugar, 2 tablespoons dairy-free cocoa powder and enough hot water added until the mixture is of a treacle consistency, then drizzle over the top of the cake.

budapest roll
budapestrulle

This roll has nothing to do with Hungary, despite its name – this cake was actually invented in Sweden. I have to admit, this cake is nostalgic for me: as a child of the 80s, there wasn't a party without a meringue roll full of fruit. You can vary the fruit as you please.

6 egg whites
(200 g/7 oz.)
a pinch of salt
325 g/1½ cups plus
2 tablespoons
caster/superfine
sugar
30 g/¼ cup
cornflour/
cornstarch
1 teaspoon white
wine vinegar
150 g/1¼ cups
toasted
hazelnuts,
roughly ground
in a food
processor

MANDARIN FILLING
300 ml/1¼ cups
double/heavy
cream
1 teaspoon icing/
confectioners'
sugar
1 teaspoon vanilla
sugar OR extract

OR use the seeds
from 1 vanilla
pod/bean
300 g/10½ oz. fresh
mandarins
(approx. 3–4)

TOPPING
50 g/1¾ oz. dark/
bittersweet
chocolate, melted
25 g/1 oz. toasted
chopped
hazelnuts

*a 25 x 35-cm/9¾ x
14-in. Swiss roll/
jelly roll pan/
baking pan,
greased and lined
with baking
parchment*
*a large piping/
pastry bag fitted
with a plain
nozzle/tip
(optional)*

SERVES 8–10

Preheat the oven to 180°C (350°F) Gas 4.

In a very clean bowl, whisk the egg whites with a teeny pinch of salt in a stand mixer (or using a hand-held electric whisk) until lightly stiff. Start adding the sugar, bit by bit. Keep whisking until you reach stiff peak stage; this may take a few minutes. Add the cornflour/cornstarch and white wine vinegar and whisk again.

Fold in the roughly ground hazelnuts. Fill the piping/pastry bag (if using) with the meringue mixture. Pipe into the prepared pan in an even layer. Alternatively, spoon the mixture into the pan and spread evenly.

Bake for around 25–30 minutes until the meringue is firm, slightly cracked on top and lightly browned. Leave to cool in the pan for about 10 minutes.

Cut a piece of baking parchment slightly larger than the pan and place on the worktop. Carefully turn the meringue out onto the baking parchment and let cool.

Meanwhile, whip the cream for the filling with the icing/confectioners' sugar and vanilla until stiff. Peel the mandarins and remove the pips and as much membrane as possible. Chop the flesh into small pieces.

Peel away the parchment paper from the cold meringue. If it is difficult to remove, brush the paper with a little water then peel. Spread an even layer of whipped cream on top of the meringue and then add the mandarin pieces. Very carefully roll up the meringue lengthways, as tightly and neatly as possible, using the baking parchment to help you. Transfer to a serving plate, making sure the seam is underneath. Tidy up any spills of cream. Drizzle the melted chocolate across the top in a messy pattern, then sprinkle with the toasted chopped hazelnuts. Chill in the refrigerator until ready to serve.

saffron swiss roll
saffransrulltårta

You can vary the fillings in this 'rulltårta'. Lots of different berries go really well with saffron, including raspberries, blueberries and lingonberries. Other fruit, such as pears, work well, too.

75 g/³/₄ stick butter
0.5 g/½ teaspoon ground saffron
4 eggs
130 g/²/₃ cup caster/granulated sugar, plus extra for dusting
½ teaspoon vanilla extract
130 g/1 cup plain/all-purpose flour

ALMOND FILLING
100 g/1 cup ground almonds
50 g/heaping ⅓ cup icing/confectioners' sugar
50 g/¼ cup caster/granulated sugar
1 teaspoon almond extract
4–5 tablespoons custard

200 ml/1 cup double/heavy cream
½ teaspoon vanilla sugar or vanilla extract
icing/confectioners' sugar, for dusting
flaked almonds, to decorate
1 ripe pear, peeled and chopped into small pieces (optional)

a 25 x 35-cm/9³/₄ x 14-in. Swiss roll/jelly roll pan/baking pan, greased and lined with baking parchment

SERVES 8–10

Preheat the oven to 200°C (400°F) Gas 6.

Melt the butter in a small pan and set aside to cool slightly. Add the saffron to infuse.

In a clean bowl, whisk the eggs and sugar in a stand mixer (or using a hand-held electric whisk) for 6–8 minutes, until tripled in volume and leaving a trail for 3 seconds. Sift the flour into the bowl and, using a figure-of-eight motion, carefully fold it in until fully incorporated. Take your time; if you knock out the air, your cake base will be flat. Pour the saffron butter down the side of the bowl, add the vanilla and fold in until just combined.

Pour the cake mixture into the baking pan. Bake in the preheated oven for 8–10 minutes or until baked through. Meanwhile, lay a damp kitchen towel on the worktop with a sheet of baking parchment on top, slightly larger than the cake. Lightly dust with a little sugar. Carefully turn the cake out onto the sugar-dusted baking parchment. Peel away the parchment paper from the cake. Roll up the warm cake carefully using the kitchen towel. Leave wrapped until it has almost cooled completely.

To make the filling, mix the ground almonds and sugars with a tablespoon of water. Add the extract and mix into a paste, then add the custard. In a separate bowl, whip the cream with the vanilla until stiff. Carefully unroll the cooled cake. Spread the almond filling layer across the base, then spread over the whipped cream. Scatter over the pear, if using. Roll the cake back up, wrap in the baking parchment and chill in the fridge for a few hours. When ready to serve, dust with icing/confectioners' sugar and decorate with flaked almonds.

easy vegan apple cake
vegansk æblekage

This cake is a favourite in our house. I vary the toppings quite a bit with whatever I have - pieces of apple, lingonberries, or other berries. It's quite forgiving. The recipe doesn't require a mixer and it's great for lunchbox treats. You can make this as a layered cake, too - simply double the recipe and bake in 2-3 round cake pans. Make an icing using vegan spread, icing/confectioners' sugar and vanilla extract whipped together. The apple sauce does make a difference in this, so try to get one with not too much added sugar.

250 g/1¾ cups plain/all-purpose flour
1 teaspoon bicarbonate of/baking soda
1 teaspoon baking powder
1 teaspoon cinnamon
2 teaspoons mixed spice
1 teaspoon vanilla sugar or extract
½ teaspoon salt
1 tablespoon apple cider vinegar
125 ml/½ cup plus 1 teaspoon almond or other non-dairy milk
200 g/1 cup light brown sugar
175 ml/¾ cup neutral oil

150 g/5½ oz. store-bought apple sauce (try to get one without too much added sugar)
1 apple, chopped in small pieces and tossed in a light cinnamon sugar (1 part ground cinnamon, 2 parts white sugar)
100 g/3½ oz. frozen lingonberries (optional)

a 28 x 20-cm/ 11 x 8-in. brownie pan, greased and lined with baking parchment

SERVES 8–10

Preheat the oven to 180°C (350°F) Gas 4.

Sift the dry ingredients into a bowl.

Add the vinegar to the almond milk and wait a minute, then mix into the flour mixture with the sugar, oil and apple sauce. Fold until smooth – do not overmix.

Pour the cake mixture into the prepared brownie pan. Scatter the chopped apple and berries, if using, on top. Bake in the preheated oven for around 25 minutes or until a skewer inserted in the centre comes out clean. Leave to cool completely in the pan.

Variations
Vegan caramel sauce topping: Bring 400 ml/1¾ cups coconut milk, 50 g/¼ cup caster/granulated sugar, 50 g/¼ cup brown soft sugar and a bit of vanilla to the boil for around 15 minutes (keep an eye on it; it needs a fast boil). Add a little salt at the end to taste. It will thicken up slightly as it cools, but will still be runny. The brown sugar gives a caramel colour – drizzle over the cake before serving.

fancy fika
& celebration
bakes

liquorice & blackberry pavlova
marengs med brombær og lakrids

The combination of salty liquorice and blackberries is quite amazing. Salty liquorice is an acquired taste that most Scandinavians love. If liquorice isn't to your taste, leave it out, and if you want to vary the berries, I also recommend liquorice paired with raspberries, blueberries, rhubarb, strawberries, mint and passion fruit. The best liquorice syrup in my mind is the Salty Liquorice Syrup from Lakrids by Bülow – available worldwide online.

4 large egg whites, at room temperature
a small pinch of salt
220 g/1 cup plus 2 tablespoons caster/superfine sugar
2 teaspoon white wine vinegar
1 teaspoon cornflour/cornstarch
1 teaspoon vanilla extract
¼ x quantity Pastry Cream (see page 14) OR shop-bought custard (around 200 ml/ ¾ cup)

220 ml/scant 1 cup whipping cream
150 g/1 cup blackberries
salty liquorice syrup, to taste (around 1–2 tablespoons per pavlova)

piping/pastry bag
a baking sheet lined with baking parchment and 6 circles drawn onto it (each around 8-cm/ 3¼-in. diameter)

MAKES 6 INDIVIDUAL PAVLOVAS OR ONE LARGE

Preheat the oven to 180°C (350°F) Gas 4.

Whisk the egg whites and salt on high speed in the clean bowl of a stand mixer. Once the whites begin to stiffen, start to add the sugar, bit by bit. Keep mixing for around 5 minutes until the sugar is fully incorporated. Whisk in the vinegar, cornflour/cornstarch and vanilla.

Spoon the mixture into a piping/pastry bag and snip the end off the bag. Pipe out six pavlovas onto the prepared baking sheet, making sure to leave a deep well in the middle of each one.

Put the baking sheet into the preheated oven and immediately turn the temperature down to 140°C (275°F) Gas 1. Bake for around 40 minutes, then turn the oven off and open the door slightly (I use a wooden spoon to keep it slightly ajar) for at least another hour or, ideally, overnight. If you are making a large pavlova, extend the baking time to at least 1 hour and test.

Whip the cream for the topping and fold in the pastry cream/custard. Spoon the cream mixture into a piping/pastry bag, snip the end off the bag and pipe onto the top of each pavlova just before serving. Add the blackberries, drizzle with salty liquorice syrup and serve immediately.

mallow fluff cakes
flødeboller

In Denmark, flødeboller are popular served at children's parties, on top of ice cream or as a special treat with an afternoon cup of coffee. Most people buy them ready-made, but making them at home is fun.

200 g/7 oz. store-bought marzipan with 50% almond content (or see basic recipe on page 15)

MALLOW FILLING
75 g/¼ cup liquid glucose
150 g/¾ cup caster/superfine sugar plus 1 extra tablespoon
1 teaspoon freshly squeezed lemon juice
seeds from ½ vanilla pod/bean OR 1 teaspoon vanilla extract
100 g/3½ oz. egg whites (do weigh them)
a pinch of salt

CHOCOLATE COATING
200 g/7 oz. dark/bittersweet chocolate, broken into pieces (I use 70% Valrhona, but a milk/semisweet chocolate will also give a lovely light result
1 teaspoon vegetable oil (optional)
freeze-dried raspberries, sprinkles or desiccated/dried shredded coconut, to decorate

a 4-cm/1½-in. round pastry/cookie cutter
2 baking sheets, greased and lined with baking parchment
a sugar thermometer
a large piping/pastry bag, fitted with a plain nozzle/tip

MAKES 18–20

Preheat the oven to 180°C (350°F) Gas 4.

Roll out the marzipan to 3 mm/⅛ in. thickness and stamp out 18–20 even discs with the pastry/cookie cutter. Place on the baking sheets. Bake in the preheated oven for around 10 minutes or until golden. Leave to cool completely.

To make the mallow filling, combine the liquid glucose, 150 g/¾ cup caster/superfine sugar, lemon juice and vanilla with 50 ml/3½ tablespoons water in a saucepan. Bring to the boil and, using a sugar thermometer, keep heating until you reach 117–118°C/244–245°F. If your syrup does not reach this temperature, the mallow will not set. Remove from the heat with care.

Meanwhile, whisk the egg whites with the salt on low-medium speed until they start to combine and froth, using a stand mixer. Add the remaining tablespoon of sugar and keep whisking. Increase the speed to high and add the warm syrup in a very thin stream. Whisk for a further 8–10 minutes until you have a thick, stiff mallow. Add the mallow to the piping/pastry bag and carefully pipe a swirl onto each marzipan base, leaving a bit of the edge free. Aim to have a good high top on each mallow. Leave to set for an hour at room temperature.

Temper the chocolate, adding an optional drop of vegetable oil to the warm tempered chocolate. To coat, put a mallow bun on a wire rack, resting over a bowl. Spoon over the tempered chocolate, then transfer with a spatula to a different tray to dry. Repeat until you have completed the batch. You may have to pour excess chocolate back from the drip bowl to use again. Decorate. Leave to cool and set before eating.

napoleon cakes
napoleonskake

Napoleon cakes are essentially a variant of mille-feuille. Many countries have variations that differ slightly in ingredients. The Swedish version is said to have been brought from Austria in 1876 - when a baker started Broqvist Bakery in Växjö. It's still there today, five generations on. This was the ultimate fika treat for my grandmother Inger. She'd never make these - few people did, because all the bakers have these lined up in their windows. She and her friends would sit and play cards, eat cake and put the world to rights.

approx. 400 g/
   14 oz. puff pastry
2–3 tablespoons
   icing/
   confectioners'
   sugar

FILLING
300 ml/1¹/₃ cups
   whipping cream
1 teaspoon icing/
   confectioners'
   sugar and a drop
   of vanilla extract
¹/₂ x portion Pastry
   Cream (see
   page 14)

4–6 tablespoons
   raspberry jam
200–250 g/7–9 oz.
   raspberries
50 g/¹/₂ cup
   pistachio nuts

*2 x baking sheets,
   1 greased and
   lined with baking
   parchment*
piping bag

MAKES 5

Preheat the oven to 180°C (350°F) Gas 4.

Roll out the puff pastry to 35 x 30 cm/14 x 12 in. and transfer to the prepared baking sheet. Prick the top of pastry with a fork and dust over the sugar. Put a piece of baking parchment on top of the pastry and then put the other baking sheet on top of that. This will prevent the pastry from rising when baking.

Bake in the preheated oven for around 15–16 minutes and then a further 3–4 minutes uncovered to give it a bit of colour.

Cut the pastry into two perfectly equal rectangles. Cut each rectangle into slices – depending on the size your pastry you will likely get ten slices. Leave to cool.

For the filling, whip the cream with the icing/confectioners' sugar and vanilla. Mix the cream with the pastry cream and fold well. It is essential that all of the ingredients are cold or it may spread out when you assemble the cake.

To assemble, spread the raspberry jam evenly across the base, then carefully, using a piping bag, pipe the pastry cream through the middle of each piece – followed by blobs along the edge alternating with raspberries. On the top layer, add more blobs of pastry cream and more berries. You want to make sure there is enough pastry cream in there to balance the bases, but not so much that it overpowers.

On the top layer, pipe more pastry cream and decorate with more berries and slivers of pistachio nuts.

honey cake
honningkage

In the late 1700s, moist honey cakes became very popular across Denmark. This is one of my absolute favourite cakes, but I can't make it too often as I really WILL eat all of it.

125 ml/½ cup runny honey

80 ml/⅓ cup dark syrup (or golden/light corn syrup)

50 g/¼ cup caster/granulated sugar

2 eggs plus 2 egg yolks

300 g/2¼ cups plain/all-purpose flour or cake flour

1½ teaspoons bicarbonate of/baking soda

2 teaspoons ground cinnamon

½ teaspoon ground cardamom

1 teaspoon ground ginger

1 teaspoon ground cloves

a pinch of salt

grated zest of 1 orange

280 ml/scant 1¼ cups buttermilk

150 ml/⅔ cup double/heavy cream

BUTTERCREAM FILLING

100 g/½ cup caster/granulated sugar

125 g/1⅛ sticks butter, softened

1 egg yolk (optional)

1 teaspoon vanilla sugar OR extract OR use the seeds from ½ vanilla pod/bean

CHOCOLATE TOPPING

30 g/¼ cup cocoa powder

80 g/⅔ cup sifted icing/confectioners' sugar

a few spoonfuls hot water

sprinkles, to decorate

a 25 x 35-cm/9¾ x 14-in. cake pan, greased and lined with baking parchment

MAKES 12–14

Preheat the oven to 160°C (325°F) Gas 3.

Combine the honey, syrup and caster/granulated sugar with 100 ml/⅓ cup water in a saucepan over a low heat until melted together. Leave to cool until tepid.

Crack the eggs into a stand mixer (or mixing bowl and use a hand-held electric whisk), add the yolks and whisk to combine. Slowly add the tepid syrup mixture into the eggs, beating continuously on high speed. Sift all the dry ingredients together, then fold into the egg and sugar mixture until smooth. Add the orange zest, buttermilk and cream and fold together until smooth. Pour the batter into the cake pan and bake for 20 minutes or until well-risen, golden brown and springy to the touch. A skewer inserted into the middle should come out clean. Leave to cool for a few minutes in the pan, then turn out onto a wire rack and allow to cool completely.

For the buttercream filling, gently heat 30 ml/⅛ cup water with the caster/granulated sugar in a pan until dissolved. Leave to cool. Beat the butter, egg yolk (if using) and vanilla together on high speed and slowly add the sugar syrup, beating well with each addition. Continue beating for several minutes until creamy and fluffy.

To assemble, cut the sides off the sponge cake to make a rectangle. Cut the cake in half lengthways and place one half on a serving tray. Cover with buttercream, then place the other half on top. To make the topping, put the cocoa powder and icing/confectioners' sugar in a bowl. Gradually add enough hot water, stirring until you get a smooth, glossy consistency. Spread neatly on top of the cake and decorate with sprinkles. Slice into squares.

medals
medaljer

These fancy-looking popular Danish treats are actually really easy
to make. The top and base are just a sweet shortcrust pastry – and the
filling is a few berries and whipped cream. You can also make the
bases using the ginger biscuit dough (see page 18) – and you can add
fruit to the whipped cream, too, for a fresher, more tart bite.

½ x quantity Sweet
Shortcrust Pastry
dough (see
page 14)
¼ x quantity
Pastry Cream
(see page 14)

FILLING
150 ml/⅔ cup
whipping cream
1 tablespoon icing/
confectioners'
sugar
a pinch of vanilla
sugar or a drop
of vanilla extract

FROSTING
60 g/½ cup icing/
confectioners'
sugar
15 g/½ oz. cocoa
powder

sprinkles and
small berries,
to decorate

*a 7–8-cm/
2¾–3¼ in. round
pastry/cookie
cutter*
*a baking sheet,
greased and lined
with baking
parchment*
*a piping/pastry bag
fitted with a star
nozzle/tip*

MAKES 10–12

Remove the sweet shortcrust pastry from the
refrigerator a while before using.

Preheat the oven to 200°C (400°F) Gas 6.

Roll out the pastry on a lightly floured surface to about
2–3 mm/⅛–¼ in. thick. Cut out 20–24 circles using the
round pastry/cookie cutter and place them on the
prepared baking sheet. Bake in the preheated oven for
about 6–8 minutes or until just a little bit browned.
Leave to cool on a wire rack.

Whip the whipping cream with the icing/confectioners'
sugar and vanilla until stiff. Set aside.

To make the frosting, mix the icing/confectioners' sugar
with the cocoa powder, then add 2–3 tablespoons of hot
water and stir. You may need to add more water, but
do so slowly so that it does not get too runny. You want
a thick yet spreadable frosting.

Spread around a teaspoon each of frosting on top
of half of the pastry circles. Use the back of the spoon
to neatly spread towards the edges. Before the frosting
sets, add the sprinkles.

Put a large teaspoon of pastry cream in the middle
of each remaining bare pastry circle. Spoon the whipped
cream into the piping/pastry bag and pipe a neat circle
of whipped cream around the pastry cream. Add the
frosted top layer to each and decorate with another swirl
of whipped cream and small fresh berries. Serve chilled
and eat with a pastry fork.

danish pancake treats
æbleskiver

The word æbleskiver literally means 'apple slices', because in the 1700s these were actually slices of apple, dipped in batter and fried. Nowadays, people rarely use apple - the balls are usually cooked, dusted with sugar, dipped in raspberry jam/preserves and eaten. That said, I think that apples give these a bit of a lift.

3 eggs, separated
300 ml/1¼ cups buttermilk
100 ml/⅓ cup plus 1 tablespoon double/heavy cream
1 tablespoon caster/superfine sugar
½ teaspoon salt
1 teaspoon baking powder
½ teaspoon bicarbonate of/ baking soda
1 teaspoon ground cardamom
200 g/1½ cups plain/all-purpose flour
1 teaspoon vanilla extract
50 g/3½ tablespoons butter melted, for cooking

icing/confectioners' sugar and raspberry jam/ preserves, to serve

FILLING (OPTIONAL)
2 eating apples, peeled, cored and chopped into small pieces
25 g/1¾ tablespoons butter
2 teaspoons ground cinnamon
50 g/¼ cup caster/ granulated sugar
1 tablespoon vanilla extract

æbleskiver pan

MAKES AROUND 30

Mix the egg yolks, buttermilk and cream in a bowl.

In another bowl, mix together the dry ingredients – the sugar, salt, baking powder, bicarbonate of/baking soda, cardamom and flour, as well as the vanilla extract.

In a third bowl, whisk the egg whites on high speed until stiff.

Mix together the wet and dry ingredients, then carefully fold in the whisked egg whites. Leave to rest for 30 minutes in the fridge.

If including the filling, place all he ingredients in a saucepan, bring to the boil, then leave to simmer until the apple goes soft.

When you're ready to cook the balls, preheat a pan over a high heat, then reduce the heat to medium and add a bit of melted butter to each hole. Carefully add enough batter to each hole so that it reaches about 2.5 mm/⅛ in. from the top. Add 1 teaspoon of filling mixture to the middle of each hole, if including it. Leave to cook for a few minutes, then, using a knitting needle or chopstick, carefully turn the balls over to cook on the other side. If you have filled the holes too much, this can be tricky, but you'll get the hang of it.

Once browned on all sides (this will take about 3–4 minutes per batch), keep the cooked æbleskiver in a warm oven until you are done – this will also help to cook them through. Serve dusted with icing/confectioners' sugar and a pot of raspberry jam/preserves for dipping.

lucia buns
lussebullar

Every year, especially in Sweden, saffron buns make an appearance and stick around all through December. These buns are especially enjoyed on St Lucia day on 13th December, and on all the four Sundays of Advent. These are best eaten when they are made - saffron can be drying. If you're not going to eat them all in one go, freeze them as soon as they have cooled.

50 g/3 tablespoons fresh yeast or 25 g/1 oz. dried/active dry yeast
400 ml/1¾ cups whole milk, heated to 36–37°C (97–99°F)
1 g/1 teaspoon ground saffron (if using saffron strands, grind to a powder in a pestle and mortar and soak in the milk beforehand)
150 g/¾ cup caster/granulated sugar
200 g/1 cup plain skyr, quark or Greek yogurt, at room temperature

1 teaspoon salt
1 egg
175 g/1½ sticks butter, softened
approx. 800 g/5¾ cups white strong/bread flour
handful of raisins
beaten egg, for brushing

3–4 large baking sheets, greased and lined with baking parchment

MAKES 30

If using fresh yeast, add the yeast and milk to a mixer with a dough hook attached. Mix until the yeast has dissolved, then add the saffron powder.

If using dried/active dry yeast, pour the milk into a bowl, sprinkle in the yeast and whisk. Cover with clingfilm/plastic wrap and leave in a warm place for 15 minutes to activate and become frothy and bubbly. Add the saffron powder. Pour into a mixer with a dough hook attached.

Add the sugar and mix together for a minute or so, then add the skyr, quark or Greek yogurt, salt and egg, and mix well. Gradually add the softened butter in pieces and add the flour gradually while mixing, making sure there are no lumps of butter. The exact amount of flour you'll need depends on how the dough feels. Keep mixing until you have a dough that is still sticky, but doesn't stick to your finger too much when you poke it. Too much flour makes the buns dry. If you're using an electric mixer, knead for 5 minutes or knead by hand for 10 minutes. Leave to rise in a warm place until it has doubled in size (30–40 minutes in a bowl covered with clingfilm/plastic wrap).

Turn the dough out on a lightly floured surface and knead until smooth. Cut the dough into 30 equal-sized pieces. Roll each piece in your hand into a long cylinder, then transfer to the baking sheets and mould into an 'S' shape (see picture opposite). Add a single raisin to the centre of the point where the 'S' shape curves (two raisins for each bun). Leave to rise again for 25 minutes.

Preheat the oven to 200°C (400°F) Gas 6.

Brush the buns gently with beaten egg and bake them in the preheated oven for 10–12 minutes. The buns should have a slight tinge of brown on top. Leave to cool under a damp kitchen towel (this prevents them from becoming dry).

danish pastry kringle
kringle

The name Kringle refers to the pretzel shape of this Danish pastry.
We eat them for birthdays, parties and at other festive times.

1 x quantity Danish Pastry
  (see page 13)
1 x quantity Remonce Almond
  Paste (see page 15)
50–100 g/½–¾ cup raisins
  (to taste)
1 egg mixed with a few
  tablespoons double/heavy
  cream, for brushing
50 g/¼ cup toasted, roughly
  chopped hazelnuts
caster/granulated sugar,
  to dust
icing/confectioners' sugar
  (optional)

*a large baking sheet (big
  enough to accommodate
  40 x 40-cm/16 x 16-in.
  dough) greased and lined
  with baking parchment*

SERVES 12–15

Roll out the Danish pastry lengthways on a lightly floured surface.

Push the sides back in, turn over and roll again. Because the pastry
has lots of layers, you have to do it this way or you will ruin the
flakiness. When you have a long rectangle of around 50 cm/20 in., cut
it straight down the middle. The kringle is so big that it is easier to
make in two pieces. Keep rolling each piece so it becomes longer and
thinner, taking care not to disturb the layers. Each piece should end
up around 50–55 cm/20–22 in. long and no more than 10 cm/4 in. wide.

Add the remonce in a line down the middle of both pieces and then
add the raisins, too. Fold each side onto the remonce to make a long
package with the remonce secured in the middle, leaving about 1 cm/
³⁄₈ in. exposed.

Trim off the untidy end bits of both pieces of pastry. Carefully curve
both pieces of pastry into thick horseshoe shapes and transfer onto
the prepared baking sheet so that the ends face each other. Join the
ends of each horseshoe together on one side. For the other side,
fold one end of pastry up diagonally beneath the other and join. You
should end up with a pretzel-like shape. It will rise quite a bit, so make
sure the holes are big enough that they won't disappear. Cover with
a kitchen cloth and leave to rest for around 20 minutes.

Brush with the egg-cream wash all over, then dust lightly with caster/
granulated sugar and sprinkle over the toasted chopped hazelnuts.

Preheat the oven to 180°C (350°F) Gas 4.

Bake in the preheated oven for 20–30 minutes. The sugar will melt
and make the pastry go brown, so do check if it's cooked through
inside. It may need a little longer depending on the thickness of the
pastry. Remove from oven and allow to cool. You can add frosting
if you wish, but I think it's nice just dusted with a little icing/
confectioners' sugar.

raspberry & pistachio tarts

½ x quantity Sweet Shortcrust Pastry (see page 14)
flour, for dusting
100 g/1 stick minus 1 tablespoon butter, softened
100 g/½ cup caster/granulated sugar
½ x quantity Pistachio Marzipan (see page 15)
2 eggs
50 g/heaped ⅓ cup plain/all-purpose flour
a pinch of salt
green food colour (optional)
½ x quantity Pastry Cream (see page 14)
300 g/10½ oz. raspberries or mixed berries
chopped pistachios
whipped cream, to serve (optional)

*4 individual tart moulds (10 cm/4 in.) or one large
tart case with a loose base (25 cm/9¾ in.)*

MAKES 4 INDIVIDUAL TARTS OR 1 LARGE

Preheat the oven to 180°C (350°F) Gas 4.

Roll out the pastry on a lightly floured work surface
and use it to and line the tin(s). In a stand mixer,
add the butter and sugar and whisk, then add the
marzipan in small pieces or grate it. Keep whisking
until light and fluffy, then add the eggs, one by
one. Sift in the flour and salt and fold. If you want
a prominent green colour, add food colour.

Add the mixture to the pastry case(s) and place
in the preheated oven.

Bake in the preheated oven for around 25 minutes
or until the pastry is nicely browned at the edges
and the filling has set (around 45 minutes for
a large tart). Leave to cool completely, then fill with
the pastry cream and decorate with the raspberries
or mixed berries and pistachios.

rhubarb & strawberry tarts

½ x quantity Sweet Shortcrust Pastry (see page 14)
flour, for dusting
100 g/1 stick minus 1 tablespoon butter, softened
100 g/½ cup caster/granulated sugar
1 teaspoon vanilla sugar or extract
150 g/5 oz. store-bought min 50% marzipan
    (or see page 14), cubed
2 eggs
50 g/heaped ⅓ cup plain/all-purpose flour
a pinch of salt
2–3 rhubarb stalks, cut into chunks
150 g/5½ oz. strawberries, roughly chopped
icing/confectioners' sugar, for dusting
whipped cream, to serve (optional)

*4 individual tart moulds (10 cm/4 in.) or one large
tart case with a loose base (25 cm/9¾ in.)*

MAKES 4 INDIVIDUAL TARTS OR 1 LARGE

Preheat the oven to 180°C (350°F) Gas 4.

Roll out the pastry on a lightly floured work
surface and use it to and line the tin(s). In a stand
mixer, add the butter and sugar and whisk, then
add the marzipan in small pieces or grate it. Keep
whisking until light and fluffy, then add the eggs,
one by one. Sift in the flour and salt and fold.

Add the mixture to the pastry case(s). Arrange the
rhubarb and strawberries on top.

Bake in the preheated oven for around 25 minutes
or until the pastry is nicely browned at the edges
and the filling has set (around 45 minutes for
a large tart). Remove from the oven and allow to
cool slightly. Dust with icing/confectioners' sugar
and serve with a dollop of whipped cream.

pear & chocolate tarts

½ x quantity Sweet Shortcrust Pastry (see page 14)
flour, for dusting
150 g/5 oz. store-bought min 50% marzipan
  (or see page 15), cubed
100 g/1 stick minus 1 tablespoon butter, softened
100 g/½ cup caster/granulated sugar
1 teaspoon vanilla sugar or extract
2 eggs
25 g/3 tablespoons plain/all-purpose flour
20 g/2⅓ tablespoons cocoa powder
a pinch of salt
3 pears, peeled
icing/confectioners' sugar, for dusting
whipped cream, to serve (optional)

4 individual tart moulds (10 cm/4 in.) or one large tart
  case with a loose base (25 cm/9¾ in.)

MAKES 4 INDIVIDUAL TARTS OR 1 LARGE

Preheat the oven to 180°C (350°F) Gas 4.

Roll out the pastry on a lightly floured work surface and use it to and line the tin(s). In a stand mixer, add the butter and sugar and whisk, then add the marzipan in small pieces or grate it. Keep whisking until light and fluffy, then add the eggs, one by one. Sift in the flour, cocoa and salt and fold.

Add the mixture to the pastry case(s) and arrange the sliced pears on top. For a larger tart, it's nice to use the full length slices – but this can be trickier on the smaller ones. I usually place half a sliced pear on each tart.

Bake in the preheated oven for around 25 minutes or until the pastry is nicely browned at the edges and the filling has set (around 45 minutes for a large tart). Remove from the oven and allow to cool slightly. Dust with icing/confectioners' sugar and serve with a dollop of whipped cream on the side.

plum tarts

seeds from 1 vanilla pod/bean mixed with 100 g/
  ½ cup caster/granulated sugar
freshly ground black pepper
7–9 ripe plums, pitted and sliced
½ x quantity Sweet Shortcrust Pastry (see page 14)
flour, for dusting
100 g/1 stick minus 1 tablespoon butter, softened
100 g/½ cup caster/granulated sugar
1 teaspoon vanilla sugar or extract
150 g/5 oz. store-bought min 50% marzipan
  (or see page 14), cubed
2 eggs
50 g/6 tablespoons plain/all-purpose flour
whipped cream, to serve (optional)

4 individual tart moulds (10 cm/4 in.) or one large
  tart case with a loose base (25 cm/9¾ in.)

MAKES 4 INDIVIDUAL TARTS OR 1 LARGE

Preheat the oven to 180°C (350°F) Gas 4.

Put the vanilla seeds/sugar mixture into a large bowl, add the pepper and mix. Add the plums to the bowl and mix together gently.

Roll out the pastry on a lightly floured work surface and use it to and line the tin(s). In a stand mixer, add the butter and sugar and whisk, then add the marzipan in small pieces or grate it. Keep whisking until light and fluffy, then add the eggs, one by one. Sift in the flour and salt and fold.

Add the mixture to the pastry case(s), arrange the plums on top and add a little more black pepper. Bake in the preheated oven for around 25 minutes or until the pastry is nicely browned at the edges and the filling has set (around 45 minutes for a large tart). Remove from the oven and allow to cool slightly. Dust with icing/confectioners' sugar and serve with a dollop of whipped cream.

princess cake
prinsesstårta

One of the most famous cakes to come out of Sweden, this traditional celebration cake first appeared in 1948 in The Princesses' Cookbook, by Jenny Åkerström, a who taught Princesses Margaretha, Märtha and Astrid, daughters of Prince Carl. Originally called Green Cake, the name evolved due to the Princesses' apparent fondness for it.

600 ml/2½ cups whipping cream
2 tablespoons icing/confectioners' sugar
1 x quantity Pastry Cream (see page 14)
1 x quantity Layer Cake Bases (see page 12)
150 g/½ cup good-quality raspberry jam/jelly
200 g/7 oz. green marzipan (store-bought or see recipe on

page 15 and add a drop of green food colouring paste, not liquid)
icing/confectioners' sugar, for dusting
pink and green royal icing or marzipan, for the rose and leaves

a piping/pastry bag fitted with a star nozzle/tip

SERVES 8–10

Whip the cream with the icing/confectioners' sugar until stiff. Spoon two thirds into a separate bowl. Mix the remaining one third of the whipped cream with the prepared pastry cream.

Make sure your prepared layer cake bases are completely even in size. If not, trim to fit. Place the bottom layer on a serving plate. Spread the raspberry jam/jelly evenly onto the base layer of the cake, then add half of the pastry cream mixture. Top with the second cake layer. Repeat with the remaining jam/jelly and second helping of the pastry cream mixture. Add the top cake layer.

Using a cake spatula, spread three quarters of the remaining whipped cream in a thick layer on the top and sides of the cake. Make sure the cake is covered evenly. Next, roll out the marzipan on a surface lightly dusted with icing/confectioners' sugar or over the top of baking parchment. Roll out into a large, even circle, big enough to cover the top and sides of the cake (around 35 cm/14 in. in diameter). Carefully drape the marzipan on top of the cake and peel back the baking parchment, if using. Pull gently around the edges to bring the marzipan down to cover the cake. Once the marzipan is smoothed over and touching the base all the way around, trim away the excess. Press the edges gently in at the base.

To make the rose decorations, mould the pink royal icing or marzipan into 2 cm/¾ in. tall teardrop shapes for the inside buds. Then roll out small, round, petal-shaped pieces of icing around 2 x 2 cm/¾ x ¾ in. and wrap each one around the bud in layers. Cut the bases off and fix the roses on top of the cake. Lastly, roll out the green royal icing or marzipan and cut out leaf shapes to fix by the sides of the roses. Dust with icing/confectioners' sugar before serving.

danish marzipan cake
gåsebryst

This cake was invented in the region of Vestsjælland in Denmark where I was born. The name literally translates as 'goose breast' – owing to the fact that it looks like a plucked goose breast because of the natural marzipan covering. There is much debate about whether the original recipe 100 years ago had a puff pastry base or a sponge base – and also whether the filling should be prune jam or another berry jam. I usually go for a cake base and berries as I'm not very fond of prune jam – but you can vary it however you like.

1 x quantity Layer
 Cake Bases batter
 (see page 12)
6–7 tablespoons
 good-quality
 raspberry jam/
 jelly
1 x quantity Pastry
 Cream (see
 page 14)
150 g/5½ oz. fresh
 strawberries or
 raspberries
300 ml/1¼ cups
 whipping cream
1 teaspoon vanilla
1 tablespoon icing/

confectioners'
 sugar
200 g/7 oz. 50%
 almond content
 Marzipan (see
 page 15)
melted chocolate,
 to decorate

a large baking
 sheet, greased
 and lined with
 baking
 parchment
3 piping/pastry
 bags

SERVES 6–8

Preheat the oven to 180°C (350°F) Gas 5.

Spread the layer cake batter onto the prepared baking sheet around 0.75 mm/³⁄₈ in. thickness. Bake in the preheated oven for around 8–10 minutes. Leave to cool.

Cut two pieces from the cake approx. size 30 x 8 cm/ 11¾ x 3¼ in. You may have some cake base left over.

Place one of the slices of cake onto a serving platter (it is hard to move afterwards). Spread the jam in a generous layer all across and then add the other slice of cake.

Using a piping/pastry bag with the end snipped off, pipe one thick line of pastry cream down the middle and then add your berries all along this (so that each slice will get berries when it is cut). Pipe more lines of pastry cream along the side of the berries and on top.

Whip the whipping cream with the icing/confectioners' sugar and vanilla until stiff. Add to another piping/pastry bag. Pipe the whipped cream around the pastry cream – and try to make the whole thing in a triangle shape. You may not need all the cream – you can reserve a bit for decoration, too.

Roll out the marzipan on a surface lightly dusted with icing/confectioners' sugar. Roll out a piece long and wide enough to fit the cake comfortably. Carefully place the marzipan on top of the cake shape around the triangular dome. Trim away the excess edges of marzipan.

Melt the chocolate and use a small piping bag to decorate the top of it – and if you want, add an extra piping of cream and berries on top.

Keep chilled until serving – but don't keep too long as the marzipan will start to go wet if refrigerated too long.

summer layer cake
lagkage

This is a great cake to make for midsummer, or indeed all the way through strawberry season. The whipped cream frosting works well and holds better than fresh cream on a warm day.

4 eggs

120 g/²/₃ cup caster/granulated sugar

120 g/²/₃ cup plus 2 tablespoons plain/all-purpose flour or cake flour

1 teaspoon baking powder

a pinch of salt

1 teaspoon vanilla sugar OR extract OR use the seeds of 1 vanilla pod/bean

25 g/¼ stick butter, melted and cooled

FILLING

400 ml/1³/₄ cups whipping cream

½ x quantity Pastry Cream (see page 14)

100 g/1 cup blueberry or strawberry jam

2 tablespoons icing/confectioners' sugar

400 g/14 oz. strawberries, sliced

200 g/7 oz. blueberries and/or blackberries

BUTTERCREAM

250 g/2¼ sticks butter, room temperature

500 g/3½ cups icing/confectioners' sugar

2–3 tablespoons whole milk

1 teaspoon vanilla extract

food colours (optional)

3 x 20-cm/8-in. round cake pans, greased and lined with baking parchment

2 piping/pastry bags

SERVES 10–12

Preheat the oven to 180°C (350°F) Gas 4.

Whisk together the eggs and sugar on high speed in a stand mixer or using a hand-held electric whisk. Whisk for at least 5 minutes or until the mixture reaches ribbon stage – you will be able to see the traces of the mixture when you move the whisk.

Combine the flour, baking powder, salt and vanilla in a separate bowl. Sift into the egg mixture, bit by bit, carefully folding using a figure-of-eight movement until incorporated. Pour the cooled melted butter down the side of the bowl and fold again carefully. Divide the mixture evenly between the cake pans. Bake in the preheated oven for about 7–8 minutes or until light golden brown. Remove from the oven and allow to cool completely before removing from the pans.

For the buttercream, whisk all of the ingredients together on high speed until very light and fluffy.

For the filling, whip the cream until stiff and fold with the pastry cream until smooth. Spoon into a piping/pastry bag. Put the first layer of cake onto a serving plate and spread a thick layer of jam over the top, then pipe a circle all the way around the edge. Add a generous layer of pastry cream filling. Top with ⅓ of the strawberry slices. Repeat with second layer and add the final cake layer to the top. Using the piping bag, pipe a thin layer of buttercream all over the cake, then smooth out using a cake scraper. If you'd like a little colour on your cake, colour a bit of the buttercream and put small blobs randomly on the cake and use the scraper again to smooth. Allow the buttercream to harden, then decorate.

almond ring cake
kransekake

This is the ultimate celebration cake in Norway and Denmark, served at weddings, Christenings, birthdays, national days, and many other occasions. It is not very often attempted at home as it can be fiddly to get perfect. When done correctly it is, however, a total showstopper. You can now buy the kranskekake rings online from specialist and some high-street shops, but it is possible to make the cake freehand, too. Kransekake is only ever decorated with simple white icing/frosting, flags and maybe a few streamers for New Year. At weddings, the figurines of the couple are placed on top of the cake.

FOR A 10-RING KRANSEKAGE

100 g/3½ oz. egg whites

100 g/1 cup ground almonds

100 g/¾ cup icing/confectioners' sugar, plus extra for kneading

100 g/½ cup caster/superfine sugar

500 g/1 lb. 2 oz. marzipan (containing at least 60% almonds – if you can only find 50%, add more ground almonds)

1 teaspoon almond extract

ICING

½–1 small egg white

100 g/¾ cup icing/confectioners' sugar, plus extra as needed

kransekage cake pans (widely available online)

a piping/pastry bag fitted with a small plain nozzle/tip

SERVES 15

To make the rings, in a bowl lightly whisk the egg whites until they're foaming. Add the ground almonds and both sugars, then whisk again until you have a smooth liquid paste. Grate the marzipan coarsely or break it into small pieces, and mix with the liquid. Your final dough will be sticky, but you will be able to handle it without getting too messy.

Put the dough in plastic bag and chill in the fridge for at least 1 hour before using.

Preheat the oven to 200°C (400°F) Gas 6.

Cut a piece of the dough and work it with as much icing/confectioners' sugar as needed to make it rollable. Roll out your first piece (add more icing/confectioners' sugar if the dough is too sticky, or your ring looks like it might crack during baking). The most important thing is that all your rolls have to be smooth and exactly the same width and height – use a ruler if you want to be sure. If you rush this part of the process, the result will be a wonky tower. Take your time and repeat anything if unsure. Keep a glass of water to hand, as wet fingers can smooth out any inconsistencies and bumps. Starting with the smallest pan in the set and working your way outwards, make 10 perfectly-sized rings.

The diameters of your rolls should be around 1–1.25 cm/3/8–1/2 in. There should be a little bit of dough left over, so use it to make a freehand top for your tower and place on a piece of baking parchment.

Place the pans on a baking sheet (never directly onto the oven shelf) and bake one layer at a time in the middle of the oven. They will need around 10–12 minutes until slightly golden brown.

Remove from the oven and allow to cool and dry before carefully removing from the pans.

To assemble the cake, first make the icing. Mix the egg white with the icing/confectioners' sugar, adding more sugar as needed. The icing needs to hold its shape, but still be light enough to comfortably pipe through a small, size-2 piping nozzle/tip. If the icing moves after piping, the cake will look messy. Spoon the icing into the piping/pastry bag. If you don't have a nozzle/tip, use a strong, good-quality piping bag and cut a small hole off the end.

It is most important that the outside of the rings look good, as the inside will be hidden until eating. Starting with the bottom ring, carefully start the flow of the icing from inside and out, just enough so that the side of the ring is covered and then you immediately pull the icing back onto the other side in one continuous movement, back and forth. This is not a zig-zag pattern, it's more of a tight 'radio wave'. If you need to stop at any point to adjust the nozzle, do so when piping is at the top inner edge of the ring. Try to make sure the lines of icing are reasonably close together.

The icing can take a long time, but it is absolutely worth taking the time to do it right. After icing all the layers separately, you're ready to build the tower. Pipe a small trace of icing on the bottom ring, where it'll be covered by the one on top. Place that next one on top, and repeat until complete.

Traditional decorations for the kranskage are cocktail stick/toothpick flags, or even streamers and mini Christmas crackers.

Tip: You can freeze the rings for up to 3 months. The cake also keeps at room temperature for several days, so you can make it ahead.

birthday cake man
kagemand

Ask any Dane about a traditional birthday cake and chances are they'll try to explain the Cake Man or Cake Woman. It is exactly as described: a cake base, in the shape of a woman or man, decorated with lots of sweets and treats. While it's mostly a kids' cake, adults do have these too – and Danish bakers often offer these made to order. These cakes have never really travelled – not even to Sweden or Norway. It is a truly Danish thing that has stayed there. It's a super-lovely thing to bake with your little one at home – and for them to help decorate with as many of their favourite sweets as they can fit onto it.

1 x quantity Cinnamon Bun base dough (see page 45)
85 g/³/₄ stick butter softened
120 g/¹/₂ cup plus 1 tablespoon dark brown soft sugar
2 tablespoons golden syrup/ light corn syrup
2 teaspoons ground cinnamon
a dash of vanilla sugar or extract

assorted sweets/ candy, to decorate
100 g/³/₄ cup minus ¹/₂ tablespoon icing/ confectioners' sugar, to decorate

a large baking sheet (approx. 40 x 50-cm/16 x 20-in.) greased and lined with baking parchment

MAKES 1 LARGE CAKE

When the cinnamon bun dough has rested, knead through. Draw your desired shape on your baking parchment – please remember this dough rises and spreads, so leave good spaces. You can choose to make this in one piece or several parts and then stick together.

Shape your cake-man, then flatten it down so it is around 1 cm/³/₈ in. thick only. Leave to rise for about 15 minutes.

Heat all the topping ingredients in a saucepan and allow to come right to the boil, then turn the heat off. Whisk well to combine to a smooth topping.

Preheat the oven to 200°C (400°F) Gas 6

Using your fingers, poke holes all over the bun dough – this is for the topping to fall into (like a focaccia). Using a pastry brush, add a generous amount of topping all over – but reserve about ¹/₃ and set aside. Leave to rise again for another 10 minutes.

Pop the cake in the preheated oven – it will have filling spilling, this is normal. Bake for around 20 minutes or until done. Remove from the oven and immediately use the rest of the topping, as needed all over, to ensure every bit is sticky and gooey. Leave to cool for a bit.

Decorate with sweets/candy and treats, then make an icing using icing/confectioners' sugar and enough hot water to make it the thickness of treacle. Pipe a face on the cake-man and outline this with icing, as it is otherwise quite a dark bake. Decorate the other parts of the cake-man with icing outlines (as shown).
Note: If you prefer a very gooey topping, make one and a half times the topping quantity.

You can use different bases for these cakes such as Danish pastry (see page 13) or choux (see page 56) or simply plain, sweet buns (see page 52) – anything goes.

breads
& waffles

Flødekranse (½
   Mel og Marg
det hele æltes
smaa Kranse.
Plade. Bages

176

Mel. 250 g Marg., 150 g Melis, 1½ dl Fløde).

...los). Melis og Fløde sættes til, og
...ger, hvoraf der laves
            ...en smurt

Franskbrød
  Margari

1—1¼ kg. vetemjöl
4 kkpr mjölk
3—4 msk. smör (1 hg.)
1 kkp socker

Vetebröd I.

(1 tsk. salt)
(5—10 kardemummor)
1 msk. pressjäst (40 gr.)
(Ägg till pänsling)

Mjölken uppvärmes, jästen röres ut.   Omkring
hälften av mjölet tages undan till utbakning.   Man
lägger det övriga mjölet, sockret och saltet i degfa-
... tillsätter litet i sänder av mjölken samt där
...möret och jästen, och arbetar allt väl till en
            ...blank deg.   Den får jäsa upp på ett
            ...på det mjölade bakbordet
            ...lig och slät, då den
            ...vilka få jäsa
            ...h gräd.

toasted wheat buns
hveder

The fourth Friday after Easter is Great Prayer Day (Stor Bededag). In 1686, a Danish bishop declared that nobody was allowed to work, travel or do anything on Great Prayer Day. This meant that the bakers were not open, so people had to go to get their bread the night before. The bakers would make these delicious wheat buns from an enriched dough. These were meant to be toasted on the morning of Great Prayer Day, but nowadays, people buy hveder in the evening and eat them then as snack. I don't blame them: there is nothing quite like freshly baked buns for evening hygge. Every year on the night before Great Prayer Day, people queue at the bakers for their buns. These are always freshly baked - but still toasted on one side. Cut the bread open, pop it under a light grill/broiler for a few minutes until the top is toasted. Enjoy warm spread with butter.

25 g/1 oz. fresh yeast
200 ml/1 cup whole milk heated to 36–37°C (97–99°F)
100 ml/⅓ cup plus 1 tablespoon water heated to 36–37°C (97–99°F)
50 g/¼ cup caster/granulated sugar
550 g/scant 4 cups white strong/bread flour plus extra for dusting
1 teaspoon salt
1 tablespoon ground cardamom
100 g/1 stick minus 1 tablespoon butter, softened
1 egg
egg, for brushing

a 25 x 35-cm/9¾ x 14-in. baking sheet, greased and lined with baking parchment

MAKES 12

Add the fresh yeast, warm milk and warm water to a stand mixer with a dough hook attached. Mix until the yeast has dissolved. Add the sugar and stir again, slowly adding half the flour, bit by bit. Add the salt, cardamom, softened butter and the egg and keep mixing. Slowly add the other half of the flour. You may not need all the flour or you may need a bit more, but keep mixing until you have a uniform springy dough (take care not to make it too dry – you can always add more flour later).

Leave the dough to rise, covered, for around 40–45 minutes or until doubled in size.

Turn the dough out onto a lightly floured surface and divide the dough into 12 equal pieces. Place onto the prepared baking sheet, spaced about 1–2 cm/⅜–¾ in. apart – when they rise, they will touch and stick together, giving them the traditional look. Cover and leave to rise again for 20–25 minutes under a kitchen towel.

Preheat the oven to 200°C (400°F) Gas 6. Brush each bun lightly with beaten egg and bake for around 15 minutes or until baked through.

rye sandwich buns
rugboller

These buns are light and fluffy and go well with burgers, especially
Biff Lindstrom. I also use these for the kids' lunch boxes.

25 g/1 oz. fresh
yeast (or 13 g/2½
teaspoons dried/
active dry yeast)
150 ml/⅔ cup
water heated
to 36–37°C
(97–99°F)
150 ml/⅔ cup
whole milk
heated
to 36–37°C
(97–99°F)
50 g/¼ cup light
brown sugar
200 g/1½ cups dark
rye flour
400 g/3 cups white
strong/bread
flour

1½ teaspoons salt
1 egg
80 g/¾ stick
butter, softened
black (or white)
sesame seeds
½ beaten egg,
to glaze

*a baking sheet,
greased and lined
with baking
parchment*

MAKES 7–9

If using fresh yeast, add the yeast and warmed water
and milk to a stand mixer with a dough-hook attached.
Mix until the yeast has dissolved. If using dried/active
dry yeast pour the warmed water and milk into a bowl.
Sprinkle on the yeast and whisk together. Cover with
clingfilm/plastic wrap and leave in a warm place for
about 15 minutes to activate and become frothy. Pour
into a stand mixer with a dough hook.

Add the sugar and mix until everything has dissolved.
Add the rye flour and then start adding the white flour
and add the salt. Add the egg and the butter and keep
mixing. You may not need all the flour or you may need
a bit more, but keep mixing for about 5 minutes until you
have a slightly sticky dough that is starting to let go of
the sides of the bowl. Cover with clingfilm/plastic wrap
and leave to rise in a warm place for around an hour
until doubled in size.

Turn the dough out onto a lightly floured surface
and knead through. Cut the dough into 7–9 pieces. Roll
the pieces into even rolls and place on the lined baking
sheet, a good distance apart. Leave to rise under a damp
kitchen towel until doubled in size again (could be
another half an hour).

Preheat the oven to 180°C (350°F) Gas 4.

Brush the buns lightly with beaten egg and sprinkle over
the black (or white) sesame seed. It's always a good idea
to keep the moisture in the oven when you bake these
– so I always add a bowlful of water to the bottom shelf
of the oven. Bake for about 12–14 minutes or until baked
through. Remove from oven and allow to cool.

breakfast buns
rundstykker

On Sunday mornings in Denmark, someone will usually do the run to pick up bread from the bakers. We eat a lot of buns, commonly known as 'rundstykker' - literally meaning 'round pieces'. Most bakeries offer many different varieties. These with poppy seeds are my version of the most popular kind.

25 g/1 oz. fresh yeast or 13 g/2½ teaspoons active dried yeast
250 ml/1 cup plus 1 tablespoon water heated to 35–37°C/97–98°F
100 ml/⅓ cup plus 1 tablespoon lukewarm whole milk
2 tablespoons caster/granulated sugar
1 teaspoon salt
approx. 450 g/3¼ cups white strong/bread flour (you might need a little more or less than this), plus extra for the work surface

2 tablespoons olive oil
beaten egg, to glaze
plenty of black poppy seeds, to garnish
butter, strong Scandi cheese and cloudberry/bakeapple jam/jelly, to serve (optional)

2 baking sheets, lined with baking parchment

MAKES 12 BUNS

If using fresh yeast, put the lukewarm water, milk and sugar into the bowl of a stand mixer with the dough hook attached. Add the yeast and mix to dissolve. If using dried/active dry yeast, follow the instructions on the packet – usually you whisk together the lukewarm liquid and yeast in a bowl and leave in a warm place for 15 minutes to activate and become frothy before using. Once activated, pour into the bowl of your stand mixer, then stir in the sugar until dissolved.

Mix the salt into the flour, then add to the stand mixer. Add the oil and mix on a low speed for about 5 minutes, then turn the speed up to high and mix well for about 3 minutes more. The dough will be quite sticky – you can add a little more flour, if needed, to bring it together. Break off and stretch out a small piece of the dough. If it becomes translucent without breaking, then the gluten is well developed and your dough is ready. If not, knead for a little longer. When ready, cover the bowl with clingfilm/plastic wrap and leave the dough to rise for at least an hour in a warm place until doubled in size. (If cold rising, leave overnight in a cool place.)

Dust your work surface with flour, then turn out the dough and knead through. Cut it into 12 equal pieces and roll each piece into a neat round roll. Space out evenly on the lined baking sheets. Cover with a damp kitchen cloth and leave to rise for another hour.

Preheat the oven to 180°C (350°F) Gas 4.

Brush each roll with beaten egg and sprinkle with plenty of poppy seeds. Place a tray containing 1 litre/quart of water in the bottom of your oven. The steam will help the buns to develop a proper crust. Bake the buns in the preheated oven for about 8–10 minutes until golden and baked through – you may need to turn the sheets halfway through. Allow to cool a little before eating.

rye flat rolls
rågkakor

These light rye flat rolls are so soft that my kids refer to them as 'pillow bread'. Traditionally, these are made with rågsikt - a flour blend of 40% sifted rye flour and 60% white bread flour.

50 g/3 tablespoons fresh yeast or 25 g/1 oz. dried/active dry yeast

300 ml/1¼ cups water heated to 36–37°C/97–98°F

300 ml/1¼ cups whole milk, heated to 36–37°C/97–98°F)

50 g/¼ cup golden syrup/light corn syrup

50 g/3½ tablespoons butter, melted

200 g/1½ cups light rye flour (type 997), sifted

1 teaspoon salt

550 g/4 cups white strong/bread flour (or more if needed)

100 g/¾ cup oatmeal/rolled/old-fashioned oats (run larger oats through the food processor to make them finer)

2–4 large baking sheets, greased and lined with baking parchment

3 cm/1¼-in. or 2 cm/¾-in. round pastry/cookie cutter

MAKES 4 LARGE OR 8 SMALL

If using fresh yeast, add the yeast, warm water and milk to a stand mixer with a dough hook. Mix until the yeast has dissolved. If using dried/active dry yeast, pour the warm water and milk into a bowl. Sprinkle over the yeast and whisk together. Cover with clingfilm/plastic wrap and leave in a warm place for 15 minutes to activate and become frothy and bubbly. Pour into the mixer. Add the syrup and melted butter and stir. Add the rye flour, salt and half of the white flour and mix with the dough hook until fully incorporated. Add the oatmeal. Continue adding white flour and knead for around 4–5 minutes until you have a slightly sticky mixture that is coming together and letting go of the sides of the bowl.

Place the dough in a clean, lightly oiled bowl and cover with clingfilm/plastic wrap. Leave in a warm place to rise for about 45 minutes or until doubled in size.

Turn out the dough onto a lightly floured surface. Knead through, then split into 4 or 8 equal parts and shape into balls. For 4 large rolls, roll out the balls into circles about 20–25 cm/8–10 in. in diameter. For 8 smaller rolls, roll into circles about 10 x 12.5 cm/4 x 5 in. The rolls should be around 1 cm/⅜ in. thick. Put the rolls on the baking sheets. Cut a hole in the middle of each with the pastry/cookie cutter, cover and leave to rise for a further 20 minutes.

Preheat the oven to 200°C (400°F) Gas 6.

Prick the breads evenly all over with a fork, all the way to the base. Bake in the preheated oven for 10–12 minutes or until lightly browned and risen. Remove from the oven and immediately cover with a damp kitchen cloth to prevent a crust from forming. Serve.

seed crispbread

fröknäcke

These little crackers are always a hit in our house – full of goodness
and they are gluten-free, too. I love these with a strong cheese.

50 g/5²/₃
  tablespoons
  sesame seeds
50 g/¹/₃ cup
  flaxseed/linseeds
80 g/generous
  ¹/₂ cup sunflower
  seeds
80 g/generous
  ¹/₂ cup pumpkin
  seeds
20 g/1¹/₂
  tablespoons chia
  seeds
50 g/generous
  ¹/₃ cup
  buckwheat flour
pinch of xanthan
  gum

3¹/₂ tablespoons
  cold pressed
  rapeseed oil
  or other good
  olive oil
150 ml/²/₃ cup
  boiling water
¹/₄ teaspoon salt
flaky sea salt,
  to taste

*2 baking sheets,
  lined with baking
  parchment*

**MAKES 16–20
CRACKERS**

Preheat the oven to 150°C (300°F) Gas 2.

Add all the ingredients (apart from the flaky sea salt)
to a bowl and stir together well.

Split the mixture in half and place one half on each
lined baking sheet. Place another piece of baking
parchment on top of each (sandwiching the mixture)
and roll out the mixture thinly and evenly to fit each
baking sheet. Remove the paper from the top and scatter
with some flaky sea salt, to taste.

Bake in the preheated oven for around 50–60 minutes –
do watch the seeds don't brown too much – until
completely cooked and dry. I usually turn the oven off
and leave in the oven while it cools, to ensure they are
completely dry. Break into smaller pieces and store
in an airtight container.

homemade crispbread
knäckebröd

Making crispbread at home is a challenge, because you really need a high heat to get the right level of crispiness, which means people often opt for the commercial types. Make sure you make it so that it is completely baked or else it will not crisp up. Store in an airtight container once it has cooled down and gone crispy.

25 g/1 oz. fresh yeast or 13 g/2½ teaspoons dried/active dry yeast
250 ml/1 cup plus 1 tablespoon lukewarm milk heated to 36–37°C (97-99°F)
2 tablespoons honey or bread syrup
150 g/1¼ cups wholemeal rye flour

300–400 g/2¼– 3 cups light rye flour (type 997)
2 teaspoons salt
50–75 g/2–3 oz. seeds, sea salt or ground spices of your choice, to flavour

pizza stone or 2 baking sheets, lightly greased

MAKES 8–16 CRISPBREAD

If using fresh yeast, add the yeast and lukewarm milk to the bowl of a stand mixer and stir until dissolved.

If using dried/active dry yeast, whisk with the warm milk and leave for 15 minutes in a warm place to activate and become frothy before pouring into the stand mixer.

Add the honey and begin stirring with the dough hook. Mix together the flours and salt. Add about two thirds of the flour slowly and mix for at least 5 minutes on a medium speed. If needed, add more flour to bring the dough together. Cover the bowl with clingfilm/plastic wrap and leave to rest in a warm place for around an hour. It will not rise much, but should puff up slightly.

Preheat the oven to a very hot 240°C (475°F) Gas 9. Add a pizza stone if you have one, or the baking sheets if not.

Knead the dough through on a floured surface and cut into 8 large or 16 small pieces. Roll each one out onto a piece of baking parchment until very thin.

Push your chosen seeds or toppings into the dough. Brush with water and prick with a fork all over. I usually cut a hole in the middle of mine, too, but it's just for show. Bake in the preheated oven for 4–8 minutes or until golden. Turn halfway through cooking if not using a pizza stone. Remove from the oven and allow to cool. Once your oven has cooled to just warm, pop the crispbreads back in the oven for a few hours to finish drying and become properly crisp. Store in an airtight container.

stoneage bread
stenalderbrød

I can't take credit for this recipe, as it is quite a well-known recipe in Denmark, and one of the big staples for people who follow a no grain diet (the original recipe was invented by a chef called Thomas Rode). I've been baking it for years and varied it to fit my personal taste – but I've not seen the recipe travel, which is a shame as it is SO delicious. I use ingredients I have in my cupboard but, to be honest, the recipe is adaptable as long as you stick to the combined grams of dry ingredients, eggs and oil (or else your loaf will crumble). This 'bread' is so super simple and it tastes amazing. I often use it instead of rye bread for my open sandwiches.

400 g/14 oz. mixed seeds (any even combination of sunflower, flax, pumpkin, chia, sesame etc., – use less, and increase one of the others – although the chia seeds get quite gelatinous so use less of those)
150–200 g/5½–7 oz. whole nuts – raw almonds, hazelnuts, Brazil (use sparingly as they can be bitter), walnuts etc.

2 teaspoons sea salt
100 ml/⅓ cup plus 1 tablespoon good-quality rapeseed or neutral tasting oil
5 eggs, beaten

1-litre/quart loaf pan, greased and lined with parchment paper

MAKES 1 LOAF

Heat the oven to 160°C (325°F) Gas 3.

Mix all the ingredients together in a bowl using a spoon (no need to chop). Pour into the prepared loaf pan. Bake in the preheated oven for one hour.

Leave to cool completely before slicing thinly (approximately 5 mm thick).

This tastes amazing with cheese, other spreads, as a based for an open sandwich – goes extremely well with a simple hot-smoked salmon mousse.

Keeps for over a week. You can pre-mix your nuts and seeds and store in bags, ready to mix with egg and bake.

Variations
Add 100 g/3½ oz. chopped currants for a fruiter loaf.

danish rye bread
rugbrød

Every Danish family has a handed-down recipe for rye bread – this one I got from my sister Ulla, who got it from her friend, who got it from her gran.... And so it goes on.

DAY 1 INGREDIENTS

100 ml/7 tablespoons water

100 g/1 scant cup rye flour

DAY 6 INGREDIENTS

4 tablespoons sourdough starter

150 ml/²/₃ cup water

150 g/1 cup plus 2 tablespoons rye flour

DAY 7 INGREDIENTS

300 ml/1¼ cups sourdough starter

1 litre/4 cups lukewarm water

2 tablespoons salt

750 g/5¹/₃ cups dark rye flour

250 g/1³/₄ cups white strong/ bread flour

DAY 8 INGREDIENTS

500 g/2½ cups chopped rye kernels/rye grain

100 g/³/₄ cup sunflower seeds

100 g/³/₄ cup flaxseeds/ linseeds

1 tablespoon dark syrup or dark corn syrup

2 tablespoons barley malt syrup

1 teaspoon barley malt powder

300 ml/1¼ cups lukewarm water or malt beer

1.8-kg/4-lb. traditional rye bread pan, greased and lined with baking parchment

MAKES 1

Days 1–6 (making a starter): Mix the Day 1 ingredients together and leave in tub on kitchen counter, lightly covered. Stir daily. In 4–5 days, it will start to bubble. On Day 6, add the ingredients to the starter and stir with a non-metal spoon. Leave for another 12–18 hours and the starter should be ready to use (you should see some serious bubbling action – if not, wait a bit longer).

Day 7: Take 300 ml/1¼ cups of the starter and mix it with the other Day 7 ingredients. Leave in a bowl on your counter, covered with clingfilm/plastic wrap, for 24 hours.

Day 8: Remove 300 ml/1¼ cups of the dough and place in a tub in fridge for next time you bake (this is your starter going forward). Mix the rest of the dough with the Day 8 ingredients in a stand mixer on low speed for around 10 minutes. The dough will be sticky and gloopy.

Fill the rye bread pan no more than three-quarters full, cover with clingfilm/plastic wrap and leave for another 8 hours on the kitchen table.

Preheat the oven to its hottest setting, around 250°C (475°F) Gas 9.

With a fork, prick the top of the rye bread all over. Brush with water and pop into the oven, immediately turning it down to 180°C (350°F) Gas 4. Bake for 1–1½ hours or until the internal temperature reaches 98°C (208°F) – the baking time will vary depending on your pan and oven.

Remove the loaf from the pan and cover with a damp dish towel to ensure that a very hard crust does not form as it cools. Store in a plastic bag to keep the loaf soft. Leave 24 hours before eating as the bread needs to settle.

swedish scones

scones

Baking bread at home doesn't have to take ages. I often make these Swedish scones if I don't have bread in the house, they take just a few minutes to put together and not long to bake. Swedes refer to these as 'svenska scones', but the basis for them is actually more akin to making Irish soda bread rather than the traditional English scone.

200 g/1½ cups wholemeal/wholegrain spelt flour
250 g/1¾ cups plus 2 tablespoons plain/all-purpose flour
4 teaspoons baking powder
1 teaspoon salt
125 g/1⅛ sticks butter, cubed
200 ml/¾ cup whole milk
150 g/¾ cup Greek yogurt, skyr or filmjölk or similar soured or strained milk

1 tablespoon golden syrup/light corn syrup
beaten egg or milk, for brushing

2 baking sheets, greased and lined with baking parchment

MAKES 16

Preheat the oven to 200°C (400°F) Gas 6.

In a bowl, combine the flours, baking powder and salt. Mix in the cubed butter with your hands until the mixture is grainy and even.

Add the milk, yogurt and syrup and combine with the flour and butter. Mix lightly until you have an even, grainy dough. Don't knead it.

Cut the dough into four even pieces and roll each one into a ball.

Flatten the balls to discs of around 15–16 cm/6–6¼ in. in diameter. Cut a cross almost all the way through on the top of each disc.

Arrange on the prepared baking sheets and brush with beaten egg or milk. Bake in the preheated oven for 15–18 minutes or until golden brown, well-risen and baked through. Leave to cool slightly before breaking each disc into four along the scored lines.

Slice open to serve. Best eaten on the day of baking.

savoury waffles
västerbottensvåfflor

My husband Jonas doesn't have a sweet tooth. In all my baking and sweet treats, he has no problem saying no thank you, and will always rather have savoury. I made this recipe one day because it has all the things he loves: a good strong cheese, bacon and a bit of green (well, it makes it all feel at least a BIT healthy!). These waffles are now his favourite and we also serve them in our café. We top them with crème fraîche. If you can't get Västerbotten cheese, try Präst cheese instead.

100 g/1 stick minus 1 tablespoon butter, melted, plus extra for greasing

150 g/1 cup plain/all-purpose flour

75 g/½ cup wholegrain spelt flour

2 teaspoons baking powder

75 g/¾ cup finely grated Västerbotten cheese (or mature/sharp Cheddar)

100 g/½ cup blanched, cooked spinach, or 3–4 frozen balls (defrosted), liquid squeezed out and chopped

a pinch of salt

freshly ground black pepper

150 g/1½ cups chopped, cooked smoked bacon pieces/pancetta

sour cream, to serve (optional)

a heart-shaped waffle iron – available online. You can use a different shaped iron, but cooking time and yield may vary

MAKES 7–8

Heat up the waffle iron and brush with melted butter.

Combine all the ingredients (apart from the sour cream) together with 350 ml/1½ cups water and stir to incorporate and form a smooth, thick batter.

Add a ladleful of batter to the hot waffle iron. Close the lid and cook for 2–3 minutes or until golden brown.

Remove from the waffle iron and serve immediately with sour cream. Repeat to make the remaining waffles.

crispy sweet waffles
frasvåfflor

How to make Nordic waffles really depends on who you ask, so I wanted to give you two recipes. The first is a recipe for crispy waffles from my mother-in-law, Eva - she makes these when we visit her in Sweden. The other recipe lends itself well as a more filling breakfast waffle - and dare I say more Norwegian in style.

SWEDISH WAFFLES
150 g/1¼ sticks butter, melted, plus a little extra for brushing
300 g/2¼ cups plain/all-purpose flour
2 teaspoons baking powder
1 teaspoon vanilla sugar OR extract OR use the seeds from 1 vanilla pod/bean
250 ml/1 cup plus 1 tablespoon whole milk
250 ml/1 cup plus 1 tablespoon water

a heart-shaped waffle iron – available online. You can use a different shaped iron, but cooking time and yield may vary

MAKES 8

NORWEGIAN WAFFLES
2 eggs
300 ml/1¼ cups whole milk
100 ml/⅓ cup Greek yogurt
350 g/2⅔ cups plain/all-purpose flour
80 g/generous 6 tablespoons sugar
1 teaspoon baking powder
1 teaspoon bicarbonate of/baking soda
1 teaspoon vanilla sugar (or seeds from ½ pod/bean)
½ teaspoon ground cardamom (optional)
100 g/1 stick minus 1 tablespoon butter, melted, plus 50 g/3½ tablespoons, for brushing

MAKES 8

Heat up the waffle iron and brush with melted butter.

For the Swedish waffles, mix all the ingredients (apart from the serving suggestions) together to form a smooth batter.

Add a ladle full of batter to the preheated waffle iron and close the lid. Leave to cook for 2–3 minutes or until golden brown and crispy. Remove and serve immediately with cloudberry or strawberry jam/jelly and whipped cream. Repeat with remaining batter.

For the Norwegian waffles, in a bowl, combine the eggs, milk and yogurt. Add all the dry ingredients. Add the melted butter and whisk until you have a smooth batter, taking care not too over beat. Leave to stand for at least 15 minutes in the fridge before using. Add a ladle full of batter to the preheated waffle iron and close the lid. Leave to cook for 2–3 minutes or until golden brown and crispy. Remove and serve immediately.

In Norway, waffles are eaten with slices of brown (whey) cheese and jam/jelly on top.

index

acknowledgments

Thank you to the wonderful team who worked on this book:
Julia Charles, Sonya Nathoo, Cindy Richards, Leslie Harrington,
Miriam Catley, Patricia Harrington, Peter Cassidy, Tony Hutchinson,
Kathy Kordalis and Anna Hiddleston.

Also thank you to Jane Graham-Maw of Graham Maw Christie.

A massive thank you to David Jørgensen.

To Live Sørdal and everyone else at ScandiKitchen.

And lastly, but above all: Jonas, Astrid and Elsa. I'm sorry (not sorry) that
our kitchen is always so full of cake and smells of vanilla and cinnamon.